Your Towns and Cities in the G

Warwick
in the Great War

Dedication

This book is dedicated to all those Warwickians who fought in foreign fields during the Great War and particularly to their families and friends who were left to carry on the fight at home.

Your Towns and Cities in the Great War

Warwick
in the Great War

Graham Sutherland

Pen & Sword
MILITARY

First published in Great Britain in 2017 by
PEN & SWORD MILITARY
an imprint of
Pen and Sword Books Ltd
47 Church Street
Barnsley
South Yorkshire S70 2AS

ISBN 978 1 47386 053 7

A CIP record for this book is available from the British Library

Printed and bound in England
by CPI Group (UK) Ltd, Croydon, CR0 4YY

Typeset in Times New Roman by Chic Graphics

Pen & Sword Books Ltd incorporates the imprints of
Pen & Sword Archaeology, Atlas, Aviation, Battleground, Discovery,
Family History, History, Maritime, Military, Naval, Politics, Railways,
Select, Social History, Transport, True Crime, Claymore Press,
Frontline Books, Leo Cooper, Praetorian Press, Remember When,
Seaforth Publishing and Wharncliffe.

For a complete list of Pen and Sword titles please contact
Pen and Sword Books Limited
47 Church Street, Barnsley, South Yorkshire, S70 2AS, England
E-mail: enquiries@pen-and-sword.co.uk
Website: www.pen-and-sword.co.uk

Contents

Conversion Tables

Please Note: It is not always possible to convert the old to the new exactly. Consequently each figure has been rounded up to its nearest modern-day equivalent.

Currency			
Sterling	Decimal	Sterling	Decimal
1/4d	01p	5s	25p
3/4d	01p	6s	30p
1d	01p	7s	35p
2d	01p	8s	40p
3d	01p	9s	45p
4d	02p	10s	50p
5d	02p	11s	55p
6d	03p	12s	60p
7d	03p	13s	65p
8d	04p	14s	70p
9d	04p	15s	75p
10d	04p	16s	80p
11d	05p	17s	85p
1s	05p	18s	90p
2s	10p	19s	95p
3s	15p	£1	100p
4s	20p		

Weights	
Avoirdupois:	Decimal:
16 ounces (oz) = 1lb	.45 kilogram (kg)
14 pounds (lb) = 1 stone	6.35kg
28lb = 1 quarter (qtr)	12.7kg
4qtr (112lb) = 1 hundredweight (cwt)	50.8kg
20cwt = 1 ton	1,016kg

Linear Measurement	
Imperial:	Decimal:
1 inch (in)	2.54 centimetres (cm)
12in = 1 foot (ft)	30.48cm
3ft = 1 yard	91.44cm
1,760 yards = 1 mile	1.609 kilometres (km)

Horse Measurement
1 hand = 4in

Introduction

In 1902 the South African War, sometimes called the Second Boer War, ended successfully for the British army. Members of the locally-based Royal Warwickshire Regiment (RWR) had fought there alongside the Warwickshire Yeomanry (WY).

Consequently Warwick, along with other towns with close military connections, knew something about war. However, nothing really prepared them for what was to come in August 1914 and continue until the peace agreement in 1919. With the memory of earlier swift victories against natives or farmers, everybody believed it would be a short war and over by Christmas. How wrong they were!

There was something of a holiday atmosphere as the troops went off to war accompanied by cheering crowds and military bands. However, the survivors were much sadder and wiser when they returned home.

Warwick Coat of Arms. (Author's collection)

In the town centre, the Union Jack flew from the Court House for the duration of the war. Other flags appeared occasionally, expressing support for Britain's allies. Once America had joined the conflict, the Stars and Stripes flew on Independence Day. The emphasis was on patriotism and in 1917, to celebrate Trafalgar Day, the Royal Navy (RN) White Ensign was flown here and from a house in Myton belonging to Mr Smith-Turbeville, recruiting officer for the Royal Naval Reserves.

While Warwick inhabitants (Warwickians) never suffered from air-raids or bombardments, many of their loved ones did and the full effect of the war was felt both at home and abroad.

Warwick Court House. (Author's collection)

This is not a military history of the Great War; however, what happened in the various battle areas also had a big impact on the home front and events in Warwick mirrored what was happening all over Britain.

Notes:

1) Where words are followed by capitalized abbreviations or other words in parentheses, these terms will be used thereafter. For example, Warwick inhabitants will be referred to as Warwickians, the Warwickshire Yeomanry will appear as WY, and so on.

2) Where words appear in quote marks, these are the words used verbatim in newspaper reports, letters from the front, etc. An example would be news from the front described as being 'better but still not good'.

3) All addresses, unless stated otherwise, are in Warwick.

Timeline

1914
June:
28th: Archduke Franz Ferdinand is assassinated in Sarajevo.
July:
Home Rule crisis in Ireland worsens with fighting in Dublin.
August:
4th: Britain declares war on Germany. Volunteers flock to the Colours.
7th: First troops land in France.
23rd: The Battle of Mons and retreat to the Marne.
October:
19th: The First Battle of Ypres begins.
22nd: First British air-raid on Germany. Revolt in South Africa collapses.
November:
5th: Britain declares war on Turkey.

1915
January:
19/20th: First zeppelin raid on Britain.
April:
22nd: The Second Battle of Ypres begins.
25th: The allies land at Gallipoli.
May:
7th: RMS *Lusitania* is sunk.
23rd: Italy declares war on Austria-Hungary. The names of the Emperor of Austria, the German Emperor and the Crown Prince are struck off the Order of the Garter and other English honours. Germans use gas for the first time, causing acute bronchitis and slow asphyxiation.
September:
25th: The Battle of Loos begins.

October:
12th: Nurse Edith Cavell is executed by German firing squad.
November:
A savage attack is made on the prime minister alleging procrastination while German reservists were being called up. Cotton is declared not to be contraband (following an earlier allegation that it was). Every 12in gun shell takes 230lb of cotton. During the Battle of Jutland 5,000-6,000lb of cotton was used every minute. When cotton is mixed with nitric and sulphuric acid it becomes a propellant for explosives, often called gun cotton.

1916
January:
9th: Allied troops are evacuated from Gallipoli.
April:
24th: Easter Rising in Dublin begins. Fifteen leaders shot and 1,200 sent to English prisons.
May:
31st: The Battle of Jutland.
July:
1 July–18 November: The Battle of the Somme. *Warwick Advertiser* (*Advertiser*): 'The great push on the Western Front has commenced and so far the results are eminently satisfactory.' Steel helmets are first issued to British troops and save many lives. Approaches by Germany for peace fail because they will not accept responsibility for starting the war, which they maintained Germany had won! Women and children in Germany are reported to be starving.
August:
'Things are going well for the Allied Cause on all sides...but the public ought to realise that we still have a very tough job in front of us.' (*Advertiser*).
September:
15th: First tanks are used. 'Progress on the Western Front may be described as slow and sure. It is not sufficiently realised that we have a very big task in front of us and it will require time and patience to make much headway.' (*Advertiser*).
October:
'The Allies have made really splendid progress on the Western Front during the last ten days.' (*Advertiser*).

December:
Asquith's government falls and David Lloyd George becomes prime minister.

1917
January:
31st: Germany resumes unrestricted U-boat attacks. America breaks off diplomatic relations with Germany but is not yet at war with them. This happens after the passenger steamer *Sussex* is torpedoed while carrying American passengers in the English Channel.
March:
8th: Russian Revolution begins.
April:
6th: America declares war on Germany and gives 'substantial financial assistance' to the allies.
9th: The Battle of Arras begins.
May:
Americans want the Irish question to be settled.
June:
First American troops arrive in France.
July:
War goes badly in Palestine. Boundary Commission at work.
31 July–6 November: The Third Battle of Ypres, also known as Passchendaele. Naval blockade on Germany reported as 'tightening'.
October:
25th: Bolsheviks seize power in Russia.
December:
German peace offers rejected because they demand no annexations of territory, no indemnities for war costs, also damaged and lost German colonies to be restored. The Battle of Huj, Palestine. Russian army breaks up and peace with Germany becomes inevitable.

1918
January:
House of Lords votes to start giving the vote to women. This decision affected more than 6,000,000 women aged over 30 with certain property rights.
February:
Some 500,000 American troops cross the Atlantic and a further 1,000,000 are expected soon. However, 219 were lost in torpedo

attacks. This report was somewhat at odds with the Admiralty's conviction that the U-boat problem 'was now held...a large number had been sunk...has been costly.' (*Advertiser*).

March:

21st: The final German offensive; Germans are only 50 miles from Paris. Allied ships and others are still being sunk by U-boats. No General Election to be held until after October.

April:

News from the front described as 'being better but still not good'. At present no legislation exists for conscription in Ireland. Lloyd George thinks there should be.

23rd: The Zeebrugge Raid takes place.

June:

Allies are now using mustard gas. Some 700,000 American troops are present in France.

July:

18th: Allies begin the counter-offensive on the Western Front.

August:

Czechoslovakia is now recognized as an ally.

October:

29th: Revolution in Germany.

30th: Turkey surrenders. Bulgaria surrenders unconditionally to the allies. Fall of Cambrai. Peace talks not going well. Germany now close to rebellion. Parliament agrees to admit women but it 'would be some time before it happened'.

November:

3rd: Austria surrenders.

11th: Germany signs the Armistice.

1919

January:

Allies stiffen terms of peace treaty as Germany had ignored some of the Armistice terms, such as not destroying their U-boats.

February:

The Germans are reported to be truculent and defiant ... 'require to be carefully watched and guarded against by the rest of the world.'

June:

28th: Treaty of Versailles is signed. War officially ends. Blockade is lifted and trading with Germany permitted.

CHAPTER 1

A Brief History of Warwick

Warwick's origins go back some 5,000 years to a small settlement by the River Avon, which was sacked several times. In spite of being fairly close to the Fosse Way, very little evidence of Roman occupation has been uncovered. In 914 AD Ethelfleda, the eldest daughter of Alfred the Great, made the first beginnings of a township. Since then Warwick has grown to the size it is today and is still growing.

Ethelfleda Plaque, Warwick, 2014. (Author's collection)

Like all towns, Warwick has had a chequered history, often influenced by the various Earls of Warwick. The castle, no longer owned by the earls, remains in a good state of repair as its owners usually picked the winning side during civil wars. One earl, Richard Beauchamp, oversaw the trial and execution of Joan of Arc. Another was Richard Neville, often referred to as 'the Kingmaker'. His influence affected how England was governed up to and during the Wars of the Roses.

Another man who left his mark on Warwick was Robert Dudley, Earl of Leicester and a great favourite of Queen Elizabeth I. The Lord Leycester Hospital, named after him, remains a popular attraction today. Dudley is buried in St Mary's.

Richard Beauchamp's tomb in St Mary's Church, Warwick. (Author's collection)

Lord Leycester Hospital, Warwick, and brother. (Author's collection)

Robert Catesby and other members of the Gunpowder Plot stole horses from Warwick Castle. However, the most important date in Warwick's history is 5 September 1694 when the Great Fire occurred. Much property was destroyed, including old St Mary's church. On a more positive side, the fire led to the growth of the early Georgian town we see today.

Visit of William III after the Fire (1906 Warwick Pageant). (Author's collection)

During the eighteenth and nineteenth centuries, Warwick was a busy route centre with a road and canal structure. Yet the early nineteenth century brought its own problems, with much unrest in England. The Reverend Arthur Savage Wade of St Nicholas church (St Nicholas), a very radical preacher, was barred from his own church because of his views.

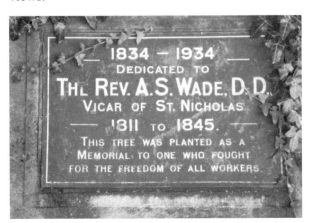

Wade Memorial, St Nicholas Church, Warwick. (Author's collection)

It is hard to imagine riots being put down by the Scots Greys when you walk around the Market Square, also known as the Market Place (Square). However, that was what happened in 1832 when the earl used every dirty trick he could to regain political control of Warwick, which he had lost the year before.

By 1914 Warwick was described as being 'a County and Assize town for Warwickshire and a Municipal Borough'. The population in 1901 was 11,903. The town had a minimum of seventeen places of worship, a market, swimming baths, common lands, a union workhouse and an infirmary. It was a centre for holidays and excursions and had its own racecourse. Concerts and other similar entertainments were a regular part of the town's life.

Instead of celebrating the town's millennium year in 1914, Warwickians ended up fighting a war that caught successive governments unawares, although there had been no shortage of warnings in the preceding years.

Today, in 2016, Warwick remains the county town but without any courts, either magisterial or crown; it has no fire station or police station; and the main bulk of the library has gone to nearby Royal Leamington Spa (Leamington).

'Visit Warwick' postcard. (Author's collection)

CHAPTER 2

The Road to War

The Kaiser had long harboured grand plans for expanding his empire, regardless of the cost in human life. While he used the assassination of the Archduke as the final excuse for war, he had been preparing for it for some time.

As 1914 dawned, Britain lagged far behind Germany in building submarines, concentrating instead on surface vessels. If a submarine sank, it had sufficient air for just twelve hours and the RN only possessed one salvage vessel for the whole fleet. Luckily the RN had no shortage of recruits, increasing its strength by more than 40,000 men by 1914. Yet, there was a significant deficiency in territorial units in Britain. Employers were reluctant to grant more than fourteen days' absence for training purposes.

In June 1914 there was a Military War Levy in Germany in addition to other forms of crushing taxation, all for the maintenance of a huge conscript army and an enormous navy. The Kaiser claimed he had to safeguard his and other shipping from the threats of an imaginary Russian invasion. He sought to justify his actions when he commented: 'Recklessness and weakness will plunge the world into the

Kaiser Wilhelm II. (Public domain)

British submarines pre-war. (Public domain)

Troops training in 1913. (Author's collection)

most horrible war aimed to destroy Germany. For there can no longer be any doubts: England, France and Russia have conspired to wage a war of annihilation against us.' Shortly before the outbreak of war, these comments were heard from the daughter of a German officer in Warwick: 'We hate you, hate you...Germany would do anything... anything to crush you...Of course we don't dislike you personally... You are our stumbling block...You are always in the way.'

Throughout this whole period, the *Advertiser* maintained its traditional policy of dedicating the front page to advertisements. Readers had to look inside to discover what was happening in the world. No headlines proclaimed the assassination or the outbreak of war, nor even the Armistice and the ultimate Treaty of Versailles; they all had to be found inside the newspaper. The first comments about the impending war came in the 4 July 1914 issue: 'Europe is startled by the assassination of the Heir Apparent to the Austrian Empire and his consort...Balkans are the whirlpool of Europe.'

In July aircraft were more effective in supporting German cavalry in a scouting role. Far-sighted men realized that the days of the cavalry were fast diminishing. Back home, experiments proved that guns used by the motor transport section could travel at up to 21 mph.

Although the outbreak of war was inevitable and expected after so many crises, its scale had never been experienced before. If the numerous appeals for winter clothing and other items for the military were anything to go by, Britain was both ill-prepared and ill-equipped for war, especially a long one. The *Advertiser* summed it up after Austria declared war on Serbia: 'We shall be very fortunate if hostilities are confined to these two powers...grave danger it will escalate into European conflict.'

The general expectation was of a short but victorious war against Germany. Nobody foresaw what would really happen. Or did they? In 1897 Jan Bloch, a Polish railway magnate and author, more or less foretold the Great War. He stated that after the initial battles, the troops would be unable to achieve decisive victories and would dig in: 'Everybody will be entrenched in the next war: the spade will be as indispensable to the soldier as his rifle.' Sadly, he was to be proved right.

CHAPTER 3

Belgian Refugees

Invasion of Belgium
The invasion of Belgium by German troops was the final spark that ignited the war. It was an unwarranted act of aggression and the subsequent media coverage was full of tales of German atrocities. Any lingering doubts about going to war were quickly forgotten once these tales were reported.

Some doubts later arose regarding the truth of these stories, alleging that they were anti-German propaganda, along with other subsequent trench myths, many of which were probably unfounded. However, the German policy of indiscriminate torpedoing of passenger vessels such as the RMS *Lusitania* and hospital ships did not help their cause.

Other atrocities included using Belgian civilians as human shields, executions and wholesale destruction of towns, accompanied by massacres. In 2001 the German Secretary of State apologized unreservedly for these atrocities committed in Belgium. He laid a wreath at one memorial for 674 civilian victims.

Corporal James Edwards of 14 Wedgnock Terrace, a prisoner of war (PoW) at Louvres, reported seeing 'Germans running about with revolvers, breaking into shops and houses and throwing things into the street and were shooting indiscriminately men, women and children.'

By the second week of August 1914, more than 80,000 Germans were in Belgium. Unbelievably, three Warwick ladies were on holiday in Namur at the time. They were taking photographs but had their camera destroyed and the film confiscated by the military authorities. Six German spies who were dressed as women had just been arrested. Later, the ladies had to leave their hotel because a German bombardment was expected. They joined a stream of refugees and returned to England. On the way, their boat was challenged by an RN ship and escorted into Dover.

John Griffin Junior of Emscote Road witnessed the Germans' arrival in Belgium. He described them as 'being dirty and exhausted, and not posing any great threat'. Yet in the same breath he reported that groups of more than five people were banned and the Germans would shoot any offenders. These tales caused a mass exodus of Belgian refugees, who then fled to England.

In October 1915, the Germans were accused of kidnapping women and using them in brothels in the trenches. A stark warning followed that such activities could happen here unless the Germans were defeated. This was at the same time that Edith Cavell, a nurse, was

Edith Cavell Memorial at Norwich Cathedral. (Author's collection)

executed for helping allied soldiers to escape from Belgium. Her execution aroused worldwide condemnation of the Germans, being described as 'the savage murder of a noble woman'.

By early 1916 German soldiers had been instructed 'to take whatever they wanted in occupied countries... No sort of humanitarian considerations have any value. There is more safety in taking than giving.' If this was just propaganda, then it was powerful stuff. However, it did not end there. A letter, supposedly written by the Kaiser, was published in January 1919. Part of it read: '... Everything must be put to fire and sword and men, women, children and old men must be slaughtered and not a tree or house left standing.' France also suffered from German depredations. More than 4,000 children were kidnapped in Lille by the Germans.

Belgian Refugees

Belgian refugees were housed all over Britain, with twenty-six arriving in Warwick during late October 1914 when they were greeted by the mayor. A fleet of borrowed motor cars took them to their new home, Junior House in Myton Road, which was part of King's High School. It had taken just forty-eight hours to get ready for them. The school took the house back in the following August and the refugees moved to Durban Villa in Emscote Road.

More refugees quickly followed in the following months and all were warmly received. Later they were registered as aliens. By Christmas 1915 more than 200 had settled in Warwick. The Misses Cullis gave twelve dolls to the mayoress for the Belgian children to supplement gifts that had come from elsewhere. In early 1916, second-hand perambulators were wanted for Belgian babies.

It was not only civilian refugees who depended on charitable donations. In January 1915 a receiving centre for warm clothing, intended for Belgian soldiers, was established at 23 High Street. A few weeks later the Belgian army called on all eligible males to enlist. Soon all Belgian males born after 30 June 1876 had to register at their local police stations. They were prohibited from visiting certain parts of the country and had to notify any change of address with penalties of £100 or six months' imprisonment for failing to do so.

At the same time, the mayor of Folkestone pleaded for Warwick to accept more Belgians. In response 38 High Street was made available for 'better class Belgian refugees'. Not all Belgians relied on charity: some gave French conversation lessons or took orders for lace-making. At one stage more than 198,000 Belgians were living in Britain.

Stories of atrocities continued when a refugee in Warwick received a letter from his brother reporting children under the age of 5 being mutilated by the Germans.

Housing Belgian refugees was only intended to be a temporary measure, and the plan was for their return home after the war. In Warwick £118 9s 3d was raised by the mayor to help poorer Belgians return home. After the war, Germany was ordered to restore 38,000,000 Belgian francs (value £15,200,000) to that country.

CHAPTER 4

Off to War

Army Pay Corps

Warwick was the permanent home of the RWR and the WY and provided temporary wartime accommodation for the Army Pay Corps (APC) and also hosted other military organizations. The APC was called 'Aunt Pollie's Chicks' or the 'Army's Perfect Cuthberts'. By the time the war was over, 2,000 officers and 40,000 other ranks handled 10,000,000 pay accounts for serving soldiers and their families in forty-four offices spread around the country.

Setting up so many offices caused an increase of separation allowance frauds throughout Britain and Warwick was no exception. Initially these allowances were only for legally married couples and their legitimate children but fraud was commonplace. The first court cases were reported in the *Advertiser* and then they stopped, probably on instructions from the Defence of the Realm Act (DORA). DORA was enacted hours after the war started and exercised endless draconian powers and restrictions.

In October 1914 the APC moved into Warwick and took over the Pageant House, then occupied by the Red Cross who vacated the premises. After moving in, the APC made various alterations without permission. While Warwick Borough Council (WBC) equipped the Pageant House with electricity, the APC had to pay for it and other maintenance requirements. This branch of the APC was responsible for paying 350,000 men and employed 200 to 350 staff. Before the war, concern had been expressed regarding the state of the Pageant House.

The Pageant House, Warwick. (Author's collection)

It was described in the *Advertiser* as being 'a white elephant and a centre of decadence and bankruptcy'.

It was suggested in December that all the wives of servicemen in receipt of separation allowances should have their names and addresses recorded at local police stations. The idea was universally detested and opposed, especially by the police. The next instruction required that all cases involving children of servicemen should be referred to the chief constable who would then pass them on to the War Office. Rumours quickly spread that the police were now supervising the families of men who were on active service. The Soldiers' and Sailors' Families Association (SSFA) was very vociferous in denying these tales.

As the APC grew, more staff were recruited, many of whom needed accommodation. Six months after their arrival, the APC expanded into the Court House. Soon they needed to employ sixty to seventy women clerks 'provided they had some clerical training before'. Staff would be brought in from London if necessary. Clearly these applicants did not materialize because two weeks later the APC changed its policy and offered training to all applicants. More than 120 women applied and eighty of them were selected for training. However, it was not free and applicants had to pay 3s 6d for the course plus a further 1s for stationery.

The APC soon needed huts to supplement its accommodation. By April 1916 the APC provided entertainers, singers and musicians for fund-raising concerts. Later they arranged and participated in sports days.

As the war machine continued with a never-ending demand for soldiers, physically fit members of the APC were drafted into the front line, being replaced in turn by less fit men. WBC was not impressed by a request from the War Office asking for a reduction in rent. The answer was NO!

Following the Armistice, WBC quickly wanted to reclaim the Court House and Pageant House from the APC. It was felt that they had been there long enough. The War Office declined to make any specific promises! WBC later invoiced the War Office for £342 3s for repairing the damage caused by the APC.

By June 1919, the Warwick Office was mainly staffed by married women whose husbands were in the army. However, as men were demobbed, they expected jobs to be waiting for them. For disabled men, working in an office would provide suitable employment and they resented finding women doing this work. Protest meetings were held in the town, where it was pointed out that some of these women also needed money to buy food. Ironically, this happened at a time when women were leaving the APC because they could obtain better pay elsewhere.

Billeting

In 1914 the practice of billeting, or lodging soldiers other than in military premises, remained an option. Suddenly there was an urgent need to find temporary accommodation for thousands of troops all over Britain. Once the barracks were full, other places had to be found. Some officers went to hotels or inns, although this was heavily criticized by the temperance movement. As the temperance views spread, hosts were ordered not to supply beer to billeted troops.

Once public buildings had been filled, private houses were used. Although the military were legally empowered to billet men in private houses, usually at just a few days' notice, householders liked having them as it meant extra income. Allowances were set at 17s 6d per week for a private, which included a bed and food. Officers paid 3s per night but provided their own food.

Billeting ceased temporarily in April 1915 before being reinstated in November. Warwickians complained that they were not being used. Leamington was full but there was room at Budbrooke and in the town. An earlier military inspection in Warwick highlighted the general lack of proper receptacles for household refuse and criticized the system of bucket-flush toilets being used in the smaller houses.

Following the outbreak of war, a great influx of soldiers descended on Warwick before being posted to other duties. These men all had to be accommodated somewhere and the barracks, hotels and inns were soon overflowing. The only answer was to arrange billets in private houses. Superintendent James Ravenhall, who was in charge of the Warwick Police Division, had the task of finding billets for them and was commended for his efficiency in this task. The Boy Scouts showed soldiers to their billets.

Billeting in Warwick was clearly back in full swing by April 1916 when hosts complained about the hardships caused by the billet money not being paid. The police assured them it would be paid in the next few days.

Fortress Company
Originally employed in coastal defence work, on 1 August 1914 the Fortress Company numbered 11,450 officers and men. Three years later their number had risen to 295,668. Warwick and Leamington formed their own company in 1915, which was known as the 213th Army Corps before merging with the Royal Engineers. Urgent pleas followed for plumbers, carpenters, bricklayers, etc. to join up. A similar company was formed in North Warwickshire, modelled on the Warwick and Leamington one.

John Henry Ashbourne was born in 1887. Before the war he was a cross country runner and a member of the Leamington Athletic Club.

213th Army Corps in training at Buxton. (John Ashbourne)

Working as an engineer for the Great Western Railway in Warwick, he lived at Watts Terrace, Parkes Street. He quickly answered the call to arms in 1914 and became a member of 213th Army Corps. John was involved in laying the network of miniature railway tracks for carrying ammunition to the trenches. During the German offensive in March 1918, he was killed at Amiens. Sadly, he has no known grave but is remembered on the Pozières Somme Memorial, Warwick war memorial and the GWR Roll of Honour on platform 2 at Leamington Railway station.

Royal Navy

The emphasis in Warwick was on the army and not the navy. However, in 1916 Master H. Harris of the Globe Hotel came 45th out of 800 in the RN Artificers exam.

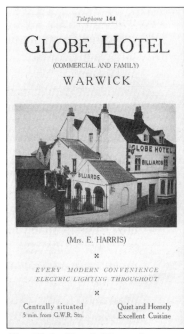

The Globe Hotel, Warwick, post-1918. (Author's collection)

The Immortal XXIX Division

The Immortal XXIX, more commonly spelt 29th Division, consisted of recalled garrisons from numerous brigades, including a battery from the Warwickshire Horse Artillery (WHA). During the war, the division took 94,000 casualties and won twenty-seven Victoria Crosses. Members of the 2/Hampshires and the 1/Essex were billeted in and around Warwick in early 1915, where they were well received.

On 12 March King George V made a secret visit to Warwickshire and inspected the 29th Division at Stretton-on-Dunsmore, prior to their leaving for Gallipoli. Members of the WY acted as escort. When the Hampshire losses in Gallipoli were published, many townspeople grieved for their lost friends. Special mention was made in the *Advertiser* of all members of the 29th Division who had been billeted in Warwick, and included a list of their battle honours. In 1921 a monument was unveiled where the Fosse Way crosses the A45 road.

The Royal Warwickshire Regiment

Inaugurated in the 1670s, they became the 6th Regiment of Foot in 1738 and the RWR in 1869 before finally being absorbed in subsequent military mergers in the late twentieth and early twenty-first centuries.

Starting in 1914, the RWR fought in Europe and the Middle East. With the barracks nearby at Budbrooke, Warwick had a strong affiliation with the regiment. The war was a very trying time, both for the soldiers and their loved ones, especially as the casualty lists grew. In May and June 1914 the RWR band played regularly at Warwick racecourse.

The 3/RWR left first, just a few hours after war had been declared. The *Advertiser* reported their departure, adding 'their destination cannot be mentioned.' The same newspaper reported that the 7/RWR was going to Rhyll. Whenever troops left Warwick, the town was always in a festive mood, especially by the railway station, with large crowds seeing them off with music, lemonade, buns, fruit, cigarettes, etc.

Far-sighted people realized how ill-prepared the country was for war and appealed for help, especially financial aid for the wives and families left behind. In Warwick an appeal was made for canvas bags to cover straw palliasses for soldiers. They had already received shirts, socks and cholera belts (these were strips of cloth measuring 6ft x 6in that were worn under the shirt and were supposed to ward off bowel disorders such as cholera and dysentery. They were still promoted several years after it was realized that cholera was caused by contaminated water and not by airborne smells.)

Recruiting began in earnest as soon as the war started. The wives of staff sergeants gave up their rooms at the barracks for the benefit of the new men and found lodgings in Warwick.

By late November the RWR was fighting at Mons. A week later 4/RWR was training at Parkhurst and suffering because their huts had not yet arrived. Immediate billeting was arranged in the town. In December Captain Bernard Law Montgomery of the RWR was

Guarding at Parkhurst. (Alan Reed)

Monty. (Author's collection)

wounded. (He would later become Field Marshal Montgomery of El Alamein fame in the Second World War.) In February 1915 he was promoted to brigade major and his standard hangs in St Mary's.

Although it was played down at the time by the military authorities, the 1/RWR was one of the regiments involved in what became known as the 'Christmas Truce'. For just a few hours on Christmas Eve and Christmas Day, British and German soldiers exchanged gifts, sang carols and played football, totally against the wishes of the military authorities.

Early in 1915 the RWR had increased from eight battalions to fourteen. By the time the war ended this had risen to thirty-one. By March 319 officers and men had been killed, 847 wounded, 233 were missing and 7 had become PoWs. Police Constable A.H. Bradbury from Warwick was promoted sergeant in the RWR. Lance Corporal Arthur Vickers from Birmingham, 2/RWR, who won the Victoria Cross and the Medaille Militaire at Ypres, was treated to a reception at

Budbrooke. He had cut through barbed wire during an attack at great risk to himself. The magistrates' court complimented him on his actions. The year ended with the sobering report that 520 RWR men were PoWs.

Regent's Park Zoo was home to four Indian black bucks or antelopes in 1916. They became the regimental mascots, as shown on the soldiers' headgear.

In January the 9/RWR 'exhibited brilliant courage at Gallipoli'. Heavy RWR casualties were reported in late April, but the location was undisclosed. The RWR

Royal Warwickshire regimental cap badge. (Author's collection)

who fought on the Somme were 'in good fettle'. One report cited how four men who were defending a trench ran out of ammunition. Undeterred, they threw bottles at the Germans who thought they were bombs and abandoned their attack. This item appeared in the *Advertiser* in late October. On 7 September 'temporary 2nd Lieutenant F.N. Cox RWR 2nd War Reserve is removed from the army, His Majesty having no further use for his services as an officer.' One wonders why? The recruiting office was moved to Christchurch School, Union Street, Coventry in 1918.

Drummer G. Scandrett, RWR, from Stand Street had been wounded and was recovering in hospital when it was bombed by the Germans. They made no excuses for their action in which 248 wounded officers and men, including Drummer Scandrett, were killed along with sixteen nursing staff. A further 534 patients were wounded along with twenty nursing staff. Drummer Scandrett left a widow and five children.

In August, recruiting officer Captain Hattrell of the RWR was sat in a deckchair on the beach at Rhos-on-Sea. He was asked to pay 6d for two chairs, but only had a note and the collector had no change. Captain Hattrell asked if others in his group would pay for him. Walter Chubb, the deckchair proprietor, arrived and accused the captain of being a 'Blackpool tripper' before he knocked the back of the chair down. Chubb was fined 2 guineas (£2 2s) and 1 guinea (£1 1s) costs when he appeared in court.

When a group of officers and men from the 2/RWR arrived home in June 1919 after having served throughout the war, they were greeted

by the mayor and town clerk and given a hearty reception at
Budbrooke. Another group arriving a few days later was received in
the Square before going to the Woolpack and then to a concert. Of the
47,500 men who served in the RWR during the war, nearly 25 per cent
of them were killed.

The Warwick Territorials
An appeal was made in September 1914 for the Territorials who were
guarding the gunpowder factory at Waltham Abbey as they desperately
needed underclothes, scarves and gloves.

The Warwickshire Horse Artillery
The WHA supplied the gun carriage that was used for the funeral of
Lord Roberts in 1914. It had also taken him to the railway station in
France prior to his return to England. The WHA were reported as
having been in action in March 1915 but suffered no casualties.

The Warwickshire Yeomanry
The WY was formed in 1794 as a defence against any possible invasion
of Britain by the French. Throughout its history, members of the WY
were volunteers who trained regularly while carrying out their normal
civilian lives. Originally only expected to serve in Warwickshire, that
all changed during the Second Boer War when some of them served in

South Africa. With the outbreak of war in
1914, the WY very quickly moved to
Norfolk for extensive training.

Following the call to arms in August
1914, members of the WY from different
parts of the county arrived at St Johns.
They used the Woolpack for their
headquarters before moving to other parts
of the country for training. Some of them,
such as William Warner Sturley from
Southam, were billeted locally. When the

*William Warner Sturley. (Alan
Sturley/Cardall Collection)*

The Woolpack, Warwick. (Author's collection)

latest group moved out of Warwick, the comment was made: 'Warwickshire sauce for the Kaiser.'

At Newbury, a stampede of over 2,000 horses included 200 belonging to the WY who were stationed there guarding German PoWs and internees. A recruiting drive was held in October for troopers 'who can ride and have a knowledge of firearms'. However, the Christmas card had the wrong Yeomanry name on it.

Some 189 members of the WY and their horses, under the command of Major Airth Richardson from Longbridge Manor, set sail on the transport *Wayfarer* on 10 April 1915. Soon afterwards the vessel was torpedoed and everyone abandoned her, leaving the horses behind. The men were rescued by a passing steamer but Major Richardson was concerned about the horses and he returned to the *Wayfarer*. Thanks to his efforts and the men who helped him, 760 of the 763 horses on board were saved but four yeomen sadly perished. Major Richardson was commended for his efforts and awarded the Distinguished Service Medal. In August he was sent home on three months' sick leave.

After landing in Alexandria, the WY was reported as 'fighting well' near the Suez Canal. Towards the end of the year, a detachment formed part of the escort for the Lord Mayor's Show in London.

1914 Christmas card with wrong title. (Warwickshire Yeomanry Museum)

At Chatby Camp, 1915. (Warwickshire Yeomanry Museum)

Turkish heliograph at Huj. (Public domain)

Gun captured from Turks at Huj. (Warwickshire Yeomanry Museum)

Brevet Colonel Airth Richardson returned to Warwick and was appointed mayor when the Earl of Warwick was unable to continue with those duties, but he was recalled to the WY at the end of the year. By March 1917 he was in France and promoted to lieutenant colonel.

On 8 November, the WY won immortal fame at the Battle of Huj which was the last unsupported cavalry charge in the history of warfare. It was part of the Southern Palestine offensive which captured Jerusalem a month later. The *Advertiser* described the yeomen who fell as men 'who fought like old crusaders for the freedom of the Holy Land… They could not have fallen in a nobler cause.' One of the field guns captured at Huj is in the Yeomanry Museum at Warwick, although it took eighty years to arrive!

As the WY was en route to France from Alexandria on the *Leasowe Castle* in May 1918, she was torpedoed. She stayed afloat long enough for 85 per cent of the crew and soldiers to escape. Two hours later she sank, taking 102 men with her including the commanding officer Colonel Gray Cheape, his adjutant Captain Drake and ten other yeomen. Early in 1956, the WY was amalgamated with the Queen's Own Worcestershire Hussars.

CHAPTER 5

Feeding the War Machine

The military's continual demands for more men took priority over the provision of food and munitions. Their small standing army was reinforced by reserves and volunteers. While conscription would have helped, it was a drastic and unpopular step to take. A less controversial scheme involved appealing for young men to volunteer or even shame them into enlisting as soldiers. White feathers indicating cowardice were handed out in London and larger places, but none were recorded in Warwick and only one in Leamington.

Boy Scouts and Girl Guides
Robert Baden-Powell founded the Scouting Movement in 1908, based on what had happened at the Siege of Mafeking during the Second Boer War. Here he formed a group of youths to carry out non-military functions, thereby freeing up soldiers to fight. The movement soon included a Girl Guide section. Their use during the Great War was to free up much-needed men and women for other purposes.

The Boy Scouts and Girl Guides played numerous roles on the home front, such as helping at the Post Office and assisting the police with billeting arrangements. Later, egg-collecting for the troops was added to their duties. Some became despatch runners and drilled in St Mary's Hall. Sometimes they paraded with other groups on different occasions, such as recruiting marches. Girl Guides collected waste paper and newspapers from anyone who sent them a postcard c/o the Welcome Club in Smith Street.

However, it was not all work and no play. On Easter Monday 1916 the scouts paraded at St Mary's Hall before having a day in the country.

In August they enjoyed a bathing parade before band practice. By the time of the Armistice, scouts were collecting unwanted food for feeding to pigs.

Conscientious Objectors
Sometimes referred to as 'conscies', this group of men came from different walks of life but they all had one thing in common. They objected to warfare, usually for religious reasons, and refused to serve in the armed forces 'on grounds of conscience'. While enlisting still remained voluntary, the authorities could do very little but that all changed when conscription came into effect. After 1916, approximately 16,500 men claimed to be conscientious objectors. They were examined by local military tribunals to gauge their sincerity. Some went to prison, while others undertook non-combatant roles such as ambulance drivers. The press had no time for them and the public was also generally unsympathetic.

Lord Derby's Scheme
In the second week of the war, Parliamentary and Financial Secretary to the Admiralty, Dr Macnamara commented about 'the many thousands of young fellows, without dependants, who have not answered the call.' He was quickly followed by the Reverend Alan Williams at St Mary's, who gave a vigorous call to arms: 'Be watchful and strengthen the things that matter.' It was aimed at everyone and not just calling on young men to enlist. A mass meeting in the Square explained the causes of the war and encouraged recruitment.

Before August was out, twenty-one men from Pickard Street had volunteered, half of whom were married. Many others followed and the borough surveyor had to share his office with recruiting staff. Another 500 recruits soon left Warwick by train in a holiday mood. This type of farewell continued for several months.

On a sadder note, the first casualty notices now appeared giving names of local soldiers who had been killed. With them came the harsh reality that war was a risky undertaking with no guarantee of survival. Notices now appeared detailing the extra number of men that were needed. A national census was prepared for 1915 recording all householders and their occupations, which established who was eligible for military service. Warwick was visited before Christmas by

'What did you do in the Great War, Daddy?' (Public domain)

a sixty-strong motor car recruiting cavalcade aimed at encouraging volunteers. The *Advertiser* doubted that it achieved anything worthwhile, apart from people seeing their friends in uniform.

WBC started a roll of honour for everybody who was serving abroad, at home or in local defence. The idea soon spread to local villages and other organizations, aimed at pressurizing reluctant recruits. Another tactic ensured the names and addresses of recruits were posted up for public view and published in the *Advertiser*. This was a regular ploy during the pre-conscription era. As the war progressed, more names were added to the rolls of honour.

At the end of March 1915 the *Advertiser* made one of its many pleas for young men aged 19 to 38 to enlist. The newspaper would supply the necessary forms to would-be recruits. In April the Warwick War Emergency Committee claimed to be the first to use military bands to help with recruiting. However, recruiting was slow nationally. The War Office knew that conscription was the means of obtaining recruits, although the prime minister insisted that there were no immediate plans to introduce it. He knew that such a law would not be universally accepted as many churches opposed the idea.

Then the Germans unwittingly helped the recruiting campaign by sinking the *Lusitania* and using gas. The outrage caused by their execution of Edith Cavell in October also led to a boost in recruitment.

The long-awaited National Register came nearer and the mayor appealed for volunteers to help gather the information. The registration took place on Sunday, 15 August and every person aged 15 to 65 had to record their personal details. Those who were already serving in the army or navy were exempt. That was the easy part; dealing with the completed forms was much more complicated and those for the district were dealt with in Warwick. There were 5,000 that had to be copied three times and were added to another 60,000 for processing. More helpers were urgently needed.

The list of all British casualties up to 21 August 1915 was published and made sombre reading when 381,983 officers and men were reported as being killed, wounded or missing. PoWs were not included and the idea of conscription was raised again. A big recruitment drive was held in the Square on a soaking wet day in early October, involving military units. Men who had already enlisted were praised but those who had not were criticized: 'Yet some of these men today are doing nothing to prevent Britons becoming slaves.'

Attempts to persuade or shame men into enlisting had failed. Consequently Edward Stanley, 17th Earl of Derby's Recruiting Scheme started in October 1915, following on from the national registration. All men aged 18 to 41 who were not in essential employment were invited to make a public declaration about their willingness to take the 'King's shilling' (another term for enlistment) if and when called upon to do so. This expression of taking the king's shilling came from the practice of paying recruits their first day's wages of 1s when they enlisted.

Canvassers spoke to each of the 3.4 million men identified by the registration to cajole rather than bully them into attesting. Having agreed to

UNDER

LORD DERBY'S SCHEME

A MERE

PROMISE TO ENLIST

IS OF NO VALUE.

If a man wishes to be placed in a Group he **MUST BE ATTESTED**

BY

DECEMBER 11th

Derby Scheme poster. (Public domain)

attest, they had forty-eight hours in which to do so and be issued with an armband with a crown on it. Men who had been rejected for whatever reason and those already invalided out of the services were issued with bands designed to prevent them being verbally abused or subjected to worse treatment.

It was a massive undertaking with the initial promise that single men would be called up first. George V made the following appeal to his subjects: 'I ask you, men of all classes, to come forward voluntarily and take your share in the fight.' Whether caused by Lord Derby's Scheme, the king's address or Edith Cavell's execution – the 'savage murder of a noble woman' – there was a

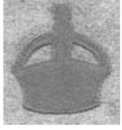

Derby Scheme armband: red crown on khaki. (Author's collection)

sudden spurt in recruiting in Warwick. Yet overall the Derby Scheme was not as good as hoped. By the end of December there had been 816 volunteers from the Warwick and Leamington district, of whom 533 were married men. It was now agreed that men who had previously been classed as medically unfit could be re-examined. Lord Derby's Scheme ended on 2 March 1916.

Conscription

The Military Service Bill authorizing conscription was introduced into Parliament in early 1916. Men between 18 and 41 years of age were given thirty days to register under Lord Derby's Scheme if they wished. Although the Labour Party Conference opposed the Bill, they declined

Romantic image of war. (Author's collection)

to agitate for its reform. Recruiting offices were instructed to recruit men who were unfit because they could be used in clerical positions, thereby releasing fitter soldiers for active service.

March brought a shock for many married men when they were called up earlier than expected. Occasionally humanity succeeded. Mr and Mrs Cox of 43 Emscote Road, both of them elderly, appealed to Lord Derby before his scheme ended for their last son to be transferred to home duties. His two older brothers had been killed in France. He agreed, adding the proviso that their son would be sent abroad if it proved necessary.

Warwick Chamber of Trade (the Chamber) offered to help businesses affected by loss of staff due to conscription, but they made it quite clear that this assistance would not be of a financial nature.

Men of military age were warned in September that 'they could be rounded up in public places' and checked to see if they were 'shirkers'. They were obliged to carry their papers with them at all times. In the same month silver badges were issued to men who had served since the outbreak of war and who had been discharged.

As conscription began to bite, what had been classified as reserved occupations became confused. The government was demanding more munitions and food while simultaneously denuding those industries of their essential workforce. In an attempt to alleviate this problem, Warwickshire County Council (WCC) arranged a substitution scheme. The idea was to replace highly-skilled men with substitutes from another walk of life.

In early November there were 6,000,000 men in the British army, of whom 5,000,000 were volunteers or enlisted men. Serious doubts were raised about how many more could be found without crippling the vital national industries, especially the food supply which was seriously affected by the German *Unterseebooten* (submarines) or U-boats as they were called, which were very efficient and ruthless killing machines. The army aggravated matters by ignoring their recruits' skills and not using them to their best advantage. They would happily waste a skilled engineer in the firing lines instead of using his best abilities elsewhere.

Semi-skilled munitions workers were warned in December that they could expect to be conscripted. New legislation in 1917 compelled employers to provide details of all male workers up to the age of 42.

Before May, men aged 41 to 45 could voluntarily attest. Later that month it was suggested that sorting out the Irish Question would free up 250,000 troops for service elsewhere. Enlisting men up to the age of 45 was breaking up many businesses back in Britain.

By April 1918 it was announced that the age for conscription would rise to 48 or even 50 and previously exempted men must now join the Colours. Clearly the big German offensive was causing panic in high places. Suggestions regarding conscription in Ireland met with strong resistance, especially from Roman Catholic bishops and priests. In June a direct appeal from Lord French, who was Irish, raised 50,000 recruits. Problems arose in August when the American government insisted that every able-bodied man in Britain had to be conscripted, regardless of the problems such a move would cause.

After the Armistice, married men were to be the first ones demobbed, followed by those who had employment waiting for them. This order was quickly amended to only allow men home on compassionate grounds. Although conscription was suspended, it would only lapse once the peace treaty had been signed. Servicemen with agricultural backgrounds were released in early 1919. Once peace was declared, demobilization gathered pace.

In June the 2/RWR, on being posted to India, advertised as follows for much-needed recruits: 'Think! Are you settled in civil life?'

Local Recruiting Tribunals
Conscription began in 1916. Those men who were conscientious objectors, unfit, in a reserved occupation or had compassionate grounds could appeal against being conscripted and tribunals consisting of five men would judge them. WBC appointed three local men and co-opted a further two from elsewhere.

In the next six months, more than 750,000 cases were heard throughout Britain. Many tried to avoid conscription, both for genuine and fabricated reasons. Even where exemptions were granted, the military often appealed against them. While not listing every application heard in Warwick, it is fair to say that most of them were rejected. For instance, a Warwick man claimed that as he ran a smallholding, it was a reserved occupation. Unfortunately for him, the smallholding was considered to be too small to qualify.

Another appellant came from Warwick School where he taught

motor mechanics and worked in munitions, which was not classed as being sufficiently important. He appealed against the decision and was told that if he could obtain an exemption badge from the Ministry of Munitions the tribunal would exempt him.

When Percy John Betts of 91 Emscote Road appealed because he had a bedridden mother, the military maintained that they had a better claim on him than she did, yet an exemption was granted to a French polisher. Thomas Fletcher, a horse-slaughterer from Myton, obtained a three-month temporary exemption. Some appellants obtained temporary exemptions until replacements could be found for them. Ernest Gitsham, a conscientious objector and assistant master at Warwick School, was allowed ten days to find work of an approved nature.

W.E. Wright of 17 Hampton Street presented a problem. He was an income tax assessor, poor rate collector and munitions worker who had been given a six-month exemption in late 1916. The Reverend F.W. Mash, representing the military, tried to have this revoked, although Wright also carried out munitions work. Mash claimed 'that it was not in the public interest that a strong and healthy man of 25 years should be in civil life…his employer had done nothing to replace him.' The appeal was dismissed and the exemption continued.

Coal-dealer Rowland A. Timms of Edward Street issued a legal challenge to the procedure and had his earlier exemption upheld and extended. T.P. Martin, a tax collector, had his exemption upheld on the condition that he carried out thirty-six hours a week in munitions work. This was another way of ensuring a supply of munitions workers. In 1917, married tramway inspector Thomas W. Mumford aged 36 was given an exemption until further notice. At the same time, the tribunal stated that it would not accept any further appeals by the military unless they were authorized. E.E. Morris, an engineer engaged on War Office work, was conscripted but Lord Willoughby de Broke's secretary was exempted.

The military lost their appeal against the exemption awarded to H. Blenkinsop who was the under-sheriff for Warwickshire. They argued that 'it was the fitness of the man, not his position that counted.' Assistant coroner A.J. Peyton was only granted a temporary exemption.

WBC announced that it would not intervene on behalf of any of its workers with the exception of the sewage farm manager and its

Lord Willoughby de Broke. (Warwickshire Yeomanry Museum)

electrical employees. Ultimately, tribunals realized that men of exceptionally low physical ability were better employed in civilian life than in the army. A.J. Lapworth aged 43 was granted an exemption because his wife was ill, provided he became a munitions worker. This was a more humane attitude than had been shown towards Percy Betts in 1916.

John Westley Stopps

As well as being the manager of the WBC Sewage Farm for which he held a certificate of exemption, Stopps was also a conscientious objector. Stopps refused to be examined or have anything to do with the army, insisting that he was prepared to go to prison. He was granted a temporary exemption. Nevertheless, he twice failed to present himself for medical examinations, denying that he was a soldier. He was later fined £25 and allowed fourteen days in which to pay. He refused and the money was recovered under a distress warrant. When he finally left his position in 1918, WBC advertised for a replacement to be paid £3 10s per week.

National Service Scheme

The National Service Scheme (NSS) was launched in February 1917 and should not be confused with the National Military Service of later years. The NSS initially called for volunteers from non-essential jobs to take the place of skilled workers who had been called up. Within days of its launch, the scheme was enlisting 10,000 volunteers a day.

Every volunteer aged between 18 and 61 obtained a form at the Post Office which was returned, unstamped, to the Director General in London. Applicants were to also advise WBC. Those who were called upon would be given seven days' notice and receive 2s 6d per day subsistence. Men were urged to volunteer. Doctors and the clergy were exempt from this calling because they had special rules governing their employment.

A crucial time in the war was approaching when every available fighter would be needed, regardless of where they lived. As 1918 progressed, the scheme was altered so that part-time volunteers could also take part.

NSS volunteers also helped to collect wool for spinning into blankets, cotton waste for paper, and old lace and muslin for use in munitions. Any profits were donated to the Red Cross.

Warwick Volunteer Defence Corps

The Corps (WVDC) was also referred to as the Warwick Volunteer Regiment and Defence Corps and consisted of men who were too old or physically infirm to fight but could be used for postings back home such as guarding PoWs, communications centres, railways, etc. There was a delay in setting up the WVDC because of delays in the 1914 Christmas post.

In 1915 the Bishop of Worcester advised that members of the clergy could join the regular army but not the Defence Corps. Men of military age would not be encouraged to join unless they were unfit for more rigorous activities. They would only be called upon to leave their homes in the remote event of an invasion. Men of military age had to be able to march 5 miles. While not being pressured into joining the regular army, members would still be visited by the recruiting officer.

Drill took place at Warwick School and church halls, and included rifle instruction. This would have been difficult as rifles were much in demand and in short supply. The mayor appealed for money to purchase equipment etc. from the army. The WVDC comprised more than 100 men and several hundreds of pounds would be needed to fully equip it. Orders giving times and dates of duties etc. were published in the *Advertiser*.

As the number of volunteers increased, there was 'a pressing need' for rifles which the government declined to provide, claiming that the needs of the regular army and the Territorial forces took priority. Each weapon cost £3 and several men bought their own but those who were unable to afford to do so felt very discouraged. Consequently, a plea was made either for more rifles or money with which to purchase them. During July Major Airth Richardson of the WY donated a cheque for the purchase of four rifles.

The WVDC suffered a setback in August when Mr H.W. Blenkinsop resigned as their commandant. The good news was that the rifles appeal worked and money became available for their purchase. In 1916 the WVDC offered to help the police in the event of an air-raid and to assist in the drilling of Lord Derby's volunteers. Soon afterwards they disbanded as there were only thirty members remaining of the original 130. The remnants joined Leamington Corps.

Young Men's Christian Association
Founded in London in 1844, the main policy of the Young Men's Christian Association (YMCA) during the war was to provide rest and

YMCA marquee. (Author's collection)

recreation facilities for troops. As the war progressed, seventy to eighty huts were lost in France at a cost of £100,000. Following the peace treaty, 1,000 were moved to villages and used as cinemas and for various industrial purposes.

The Warwick Branch was established on 24 January 1918 at Abbotsford House in the Square and soon became involved in fund-raising for huts, dugouts, etc. for the troops fighting abroad. Within days of opening, the branch had raised £1,254 4s including £59 that was sent to the central fund.

Abbotsford House, site of YMCA. (John Ashbourne)

CHAPTER 6

The War in the Air and at Sea

In the Air

Unlike other parts of the country, aerial warfare did not really affect Warwick. Many Warwickians had their first experience of aircraft in 1915 when two planes attached to the Royal Field Artillery flew over the area.

However, as air-raids increased, Warwickshire's Chief Constable, Captain John Brinkley, issued advice. He described it as a 'Precautionary Scheme in the possible event of an AIR-CRAFT RAID [*sic*]', adding that cellars offered the best refuge: 'People should stay indoors. If the raid was in the night time, then all lights were to be extinguished. Street lights were to be kept to a minimum, and if necessary, extinguished. Warnings would be given by the use of syrens [*sic*], hooters, gong or bells.' The notice stressed that these were 'merely precautionary measures'. Two Warwick boys spent their Easter holidays in Suffolk, collecting shrapnel and bomb parts. There was an air-raid while they were there but they somehow slept through it!

The General Accident Fire & Life Assurance Company Ltd (London & Scotland) was quick to offer policies that included zeppelin risks. The Warwick Board of Guardians (BoG), who oversaw the running of the workhouse, declined such insurance. Workhouses originally provided accommodation and employment for those who were unable to find work and they employed harsh regimes to deter malingerers. The Warwick workhouse became an infirmary in 1930

Royal Flying Corps poster. (Public domain)

and later part of Warwick hospital but all the old workhouse buildings have since been demolished.

During the first week of 1916, lights from houses were to be blacked out, allowing only a dull subdued light to be visible from the outside. The instructions were unpopular and within weeks six Warwickians were successfully prosecuted for ignoring them. Zeppelin raids occurred in the Midlands. The chief constable of Birmingham resisted removing the ban only days before the blackout foiled a raid on the city.

Suggestions to build an aerodrome on Warwick Common came to nothing. Warwick did not have any anti-aircraft batteries because there was no real industry in the area; consequently the chief constable insisted that the only real protection from air-raids was to show no lights. House windows needed blinds or other forms of blackout and street lights were obscured or extinguished; advance warnings of a raid could not be expected. Conscious of the growing risk of air-raids, a further eighteen special constables were appointed to help with these duties. It was decided not to use sirens in case they encouraged people out into the streets. By December, the fire brigade turned out if zeppelins were reported in the area. Sand was stockpiled because water was known to be of no use against fires caused by incendiaries. Due to the blackout, the local churches would finish evensong before it got dark.

In March 1918, the media reported that Germany was receiving more air-raids than the allies. In August an air-raid was rumoured as being about to happen over Warwick, although the fire brigade and police knew nothing about it. Residents panicked and began shouting and kicking doors. When sanity returned, it was discovered that the air-raid in question was 150 miles away! In spite of air-raids happening over England, criticism of the blackout continued, claiming it was purely an economy measure and nothing to do with air-raids. Warwick finally saw an airship, the R33, when it flew over the town during the official peace celebrations in July 1919.

At Sea

In spite of Britain having a formidable navy, the Germans almost ruled the waves with their U-boats, which might have won the war for them. However, their declaration of unrestricted warfare against any ships, including neutrals, suspected of trading with Britain contributed to their ultimate defeat.

The first warning of unrestricted warfare came in early 1915. Others followed, which angered neutral countries of the time, especially America. While the RN could successfully blockade German ports, dealing with the U-boats was a different story. There was a growing opinion that U-boats sinking unarmed ships turned German sailors into pirates, who should be treated as such when captured and not as PoWs.

Torpedoes were expensive, so U-boats generally preferred to

destroy merchant ships on the surface. The ships were boarded and either scuttled or sunk by gunfire after the passengers had been evacuated. While making good economic sense, it disclosed a U-boat's weakness. By late 1914 decoy vessels known as Q-ships had been created by Britain: these resembled unarmed merchant ships but were in fact armed and would tackle U-boats while the latter were on the surface. U-boats consequently became more cautious and developed their own devious tricks. The success of the Q-ships has been greatly overrated and they only accounted for approximately 10 per cent of the U-boats sunk.

Warwickians did not worry too much about the war at sea until the sinking of the *Wayfarer* and the RMS *Lusitania*, both of which had local connections. The *Lusitania* sinking on 7 May 1915 off the Irish Coast caused a massive anti-German backlash throughout the world. The vessel was a powerful ocean liner carrying nearly 2,000 passengers but at the time of her loss her captain was only travelling at 20 kph, less than half her maximum speed, and instead of sailing on a zigzag course she went straight and was hit by a single torpedo. She sank along with some 1,200 passengers, many of whom were American citizens. While this

Lusitania-sinking German medal. (Author's collection)

barbarous act did not bring America into the war, it certainly did the German cause no good. There were great celebrations in Germany when the news was heard and they even issued the *Lusitania* medal to celebrate the event.

An inquest held on the bodies returned a verdict of 'Wilful and wholesale murder'. Germany might have rejoiced at the news, but it was a pyrrhic victory as the incident caused a massive increase in men joining the British army. Two ladies from Kenilworth were killed, while a man from Leamington survived. However, the *Lusitania*'s chief officer Mr J.S. Piper, who lived in Emscote Road, died at his post 'doing his duty like the brave soul he was'.

Anti-German feelings following the *Lusitania* sinking did not deter the Germans from committing other barbaric acts because they believed that their actions were legitimate. On 30 December 1915, the SS *Persia* was torpedoed, without warning, off Crete. Among the fatalities was Mrs Stoehr of Stratford-upon-Avon, who was a niece of Mr R. Dudley of Warwick.

The naval Battle of Jutland on 31 May 1916 sealed Britain's control of the seas for the rest of the war, except for the U-boats. What should have been a clear victory was indecisive until the German navy fled. Britain lost 14 ships and 6,000 men, while Germany lost 10 ships and 2,400 men. Was it a glorious victory or a defeat? Among the British losses was Sub-Lieutenant the Honourable Algernon William Percy RNR, only son and heir of Lord Algernon Percy of Guy's Cliffe. He was serving on HMS *Queen Mary*. Also killed was William Eden on HMS *Indefatigable*. His brother was future prime minister Antony Eden, who had married the Countess of Warwick's daughter's stepdaughter. Both ships were sunk.

Only five days later, Secretary of State for War Lord Kitchener was killed when his ship HMS *Hampshire* struck a mine off the Orkneys. He remained a cult figure, regardless of his abilities, and is best remembered for his famous recruiting campaigns and posters. His death shocked the nation.

German U-boats continued sinking any vessel they considered to be an enemy, even including hospital ships. The government now realized that the RN's dependence on dreadnought battleships was vastly overrated. These had much heavier-calibre guns than before and used steam turbines, but Germany was producing new U-boats every week. At last these vessels were recognized as a major threat to Britain's supply lines. As 1916 came to an end, shipbuilding was hindered by the number of qualified engineers who had been conscripted. During one week in April 1917, sixty-four ships were sunk which was the largest number on record and resulted in a great loss of lives and food supplies.

For two Warwick families, early July 1917 brought them good news. Private John Mitchell from Parkes Street and Private Ayton from Emscote Road had been on the RMS *Transylvania* which was carrying troops to Egypt. She was torpedoed on 4 May with heavy loss of life; however, these two men were reported as safe.

Even hospital ships such as the HMHS *Rewa* were attacked, in contravention of the Hague Convention. The *Rewa* was sunk in January

HMHS Rewa. *(Public domain)*

HMS Warwick. *(Public domain)*

1918, although this act was denied by Germany. The U-boat commander Wilhelm Werner was wanted for war crimes but he disappeared. No wonder many people wanted to treat captured German submariners as pirates. Even while peace talks were taking place in October, a U-boat sank an Irish mail boat, killing 600 people.

HMS *Warwick*

HMS *Warwick*, an Admiralty 'W'-class destroyer, was in commission by March 1918. Her commander was anxious to display the town's coat of arms on his ship and the town happily obliged. In return, her old ensign was given to Warwick. She took part in the Zeebrugge Raid and was later damaged at Ostend but after repair returned to sea. In March 1942, HMS *Warwick* was adopted by Warwickians. She was torpedoed in February 1944 with the loss of half her crew.

CHAPTER 7

Transport at Home and Abroad

Canals

Since being built, the Warwick-Napton canal system in Warwick has caused many deaths, either accidental or deliberate. Where drownings were clearly suicides, the inquest jury usually added a rider that the victim was suffering from 'temporary insanity', thereby negating the suicide stigma.

In late October 1914, while he was about to be interviewed by PC Percy Watts, Private Thomas Johnson of the Army Service Corps tried to cut his throat. When that failed, he was chased by PC Watts towards the Cape where he jumped into the canal. Here it was very deep and about 40ft wide. PC Watts dived into the canal and rescued him. He was later awarded a Certificate on Vellum from the Humane Society for his action. Yet the chief constable had to obtain permission from the Standing Joint Committee (SJC), who oversaw the running of the police, to replace the constable's watch which had been ruined in the canal. Johnson had two wounds to his throat and a further two to his stomach. Once his injuries had been treated, he was detained in the workhouse infirmary but later discharged.

Little Eva Frances Smith drowned in 1917 while playing with a young boy who was too scared to raise the alarm. They had already been moved away by a police officer but then went back. Charlotte Annie Canning, wife of Alfred Canning of 24 Packmore Street, drowned herself. She was deaf and suffered from various delusions.

Her body was first seen by rag-and-bone dealer George Hewitt. He made no attempt to help but stole her clothes instead which she had left on the canal bank.

Trains

In 1914 as the world moved steadily towards war, life went on as normal in Warwick with excursions planned to visit the Isle of Man, Liverpool and London. Not all midday trains stopped at Warwick; this was at a time when the town wanted to extend its holiday facilities.

When war broke out, the railways were very busy moving troops around. After a brief lull, life returned to normal and by the end of August cheap excursions were offered once more, albeit not for long. The railways still had a big part to play in moving troops and wounded men around the country. Likewise, at the end of the war they had a similar role in bringing the troops home.

Early 1915 saw a big recruiting campaign for drivers to join the Mechanical Transport Army Service Corps for the duration of the war. Locally successful applicants obtained railway travel warrants from WBC. In late March, no trains ran for two days after heavy snowstorms that were described as 'the worst in living memory'. As the year progressed, fewer trains were available to convey munitions workers to Coventry.

Warwick railway station. (Author's collection)

By 1916 the railway services were reduced and fares increased by 50 per cent. Workmen's tickets were exempt up to a 40-mile radius. The Warwick Corn Exchange only opened from 2 pm to 3 pm during the Saturday markets. Further restrictions followed in 1918, when trains were limited to 35 mph. By mid-August people needed a permit to authorize their travel in very few crowded carriages. This was a deliberate ploy to discourage travel.

In late October John Smith, a discharged soldier from 12 Linen Street, was fined £1 10s for travelling to Coventry without a ticket. (I once lived in the more modern 12 Linen Street, built on the site of the old one.) During the night of 29 January 1919, Richard Henry Hadden aged 47 lay down in front of a train near St Mary's Common. The inquest jury returned a verdict of taking his own life while being 'temporarily insane'. He had tried to kill himself before.

Railwaymen won few friends with their threatened strike actions for more money and shorter hours. Yet compared to the life of a fighting man in the trenches, they had an easy time. Many people thought that if they continued to strike, then they should be drafted into the army. To be fair, many railwaymen did enlist, with some of them paying the ultimate price.

Roads

Complaints about the state of the roads are nothing new. Before the war, people and the media complained about the road from Warwick to Guy's Cliffe being full of holes. Similar complaints followed about the Emscote Road and Stratford Road. By 1919 nothing had been done about it and Airth Richardson complained to WCC.

Further complaints followed about the tram tracks along Emscote Road, Coten End, Smith Street, Jury Street and High Street, for which the Leamington & Warwick Electrical Co. Ltd (the tram company), formerly Leamington & Warwick Tramways & Omnibus Co. was blamed. In their turn they blamed the railway for the water that dripped from the Emscote Road railway bridge. These remained a cause for concern until January 1919, when the borough surveyor took the matter up with WCC. At the same time, the tram company started relaying the track in Emscote Road, which remedied that particular problem. The area in and around the Square was also heavily criticized.

These were not the only roads in a poor state of repair. The state of the roads and the tram tracks brought regular complaints both to and from WBC. In August 1917 WCC stated that they had spent £422 between 1 April 1913 and 31 March 1917 on repairs. Their poor performance was blamed on a shortage of men and materials.

On 4 November 1914 Charles Henry Parr, an inmate of the workhouse, received fatal injuries in Lakin Road when he collided with a bicycle. The inquest jury put much of the blame on the bad state of the road. A letter from a member of the APC was published in December by the *Advertiser*. The writer had seen a large road-sweeper removing mud from Coten End. He felt this was a 'distinct feature of the roads around Warwick... such an unusual occurrence... had to write to the paper.' Was he being sarcastic?

Horses

The first few years of the twentieth century brought forth many changes, especially in transport. Motor vehicles and bicycles increased in ownership and brought new laws with them. Public transport moved on from being horse-drawn to electrically-powered. In 1919 WBC and other organizations started thinking about using mechanical vehicles instead of horses.

Meanwhile, there was still a great need for these particular animals. Farmers who could not afford to buy or hire mechanized vehicles depended on horses for numerous tasks and it was the same with the military. Apart from specific mounted regiments, hundreds of thousands of horses were needed for a wide variety of transport purposes. Motor vehicles had their uses but horses and mules were better for moving over rough ground. During the next few years the number of horses required rose dramatically and they were conscripted in a similar manner to men from back home.

Somewhere in the region of 6,000,000 horses and mules were used in this way. The British army lost nearly 500,000 horses during the war to exhaustion, disease, wounds, gassing and shellshock. More than half of them died on the Western Front as, just like the ordinary soldiers, they faced the same dangers. On the one hand they were great morale-boosters to the troops but they also helped to spread disease. The British Veterinary Corps did amazing work both on and off the battlefields and treated over 700,000 casualties, saving about 70 per cent of them.

By 8 August 1914, horses were already being commandeered.

Kitchener initially decreed that only animals with a minimum height of 15 hands (60in or 152cm) were to be taken. However, these limits were soon to be reduced or ignored.

One week later, men, supplies and horses gathered in Warwick Castle Park, the Common and Margetts Sale Yards, but not always without incident. For example, Arthur Townsend, a trooper in the Gloucestershire Yeomanry, had his jaw broken by a kicking horse.

The War Office learned a valuable lesson from the Second Boer War of 1899–1902 when horse fraud was rife. The *Advertiser* named the only six men who were empowered in Warwickshire to purchase horses for the army. Anybody else attempting to do so should be reported to the police.

WBC voluntarily surrendered three of its draught horses to the army. A few weeks later they purchased another two animals for £174. If they had hoped to appease the army, they failed. A month later the army requisitioned a further five beasts from them. By 1919, a new horse cost £140.

On New Year's Eve John Gardner, a drunken farmer, drove his horse and cart along the middle of the Banbury Road, collided with another horse and overturned his cart. He was later fined £1.

In January 1915, conscious of the suffering of animals at the front, what was described as 'a patriotic entertainment' was held at the Nelson Hall. Sweets were sold during the interval and the money raised was forwarded to the Purple Cross Service designed especially for the treatment of wounded horses. It was one thing taking thousands of horses into military service, but who was going to look after them? In late February 'Skilled Shoeing Smiths were wanted urgently by the army.' Applicants had to be fit and under 45 years of age. The pay offered was 5s per day plus a separation allowance. This advert was repeated in early April.

While the war caused many events to be cancelled, the Shire Horse Society still held their second annual show at the Punch Bowl on 27 March. The third followed in 1916 at the nearby Priory Fields, followed by a cold lunch in the Punch Bowl. However, the show was cancelled in 1917.

Meanwhile, replacement mounts and heavy draught animals for pulling artillery were now urgently required. The War Office guaranteed to pay 'full value' for riding cobs that were 'quiet to ride and with good mouths'. Strong polo ponies were considered to be ideal. In late June, rumours quickly spread around Warwick about military horses being ill-treated in Leamington. Some animals had been injured but there was no evidence of them having been abused.

By March 1917, the War Office had purchased more than 400,000 horses at a cost of £20,000,000, or on average £50 per horse. This meant fewer horses to work on the land. Mr W.J. Lees from Heathcote quickly offered his Shire colt 'Friars Champion' to service local mares for just £3 3s plus 12s 6d for the groom.

However, the military overlooked a very important matter when conscripting all these animals. Officers and cavalrymen had their own mounts, but who would drive all the other beasts that were needed for supply purposes? By the middle of May, the Royal Army Service Corps 'urgently' wanted men aged 41 to 60 with riding experience to sign up for duty in the remount depots. These volunteers had to weigh less than 14 stone 'and not suffer from ruptures or from anything that would prevent equitation'.

By 1 October, the Leamington and Warwick National Master Farriers Association raised the cost of shoeing horses with immediate effect. They blamed the 'unprecedented rise in the costs of raw materials'. There was no let-up in the war hardships and the March, June and August 1918 meetings of Warwick Races were cancelled. Although there were enough horses to race, the railways could not provide any trains because of limited coal supplies. The races would not be revived until after the Armistice when the trains were able to run more frequently.

Once the Armistice had been signed, most people believed that the war was over, although the peace treaty would not be signed for several more months. There was much less demand for horses by the military; they became much cheaper to purchase and licences were no longer needed. Since 1914 their price had risen by 80 per cent and in December the military began selling off 75,000 horses. During the war, the military had taken 17.5 per cent of all available horses in Britain and now wanted to return some of them. Over a three-week period, 100 horses went to the cities and 125 to the towns. The Board of Agriculture was willing to place 'light army mares' with farmers at an annual rent of £2 for breeding purposes.

Crown Hotel, St John's at Coventry Road, Warwick. (Author's collection)

Bicycles and Motorcycles

Bicycles were used by civilians and military personnel alike. No doubt the tram tracks would have been quite a hazard. Members of the RWR had their own bicycles and used them in 1891 to chase someone who had robbed one of their wives. D. Hackleton traded from Smith Street and Priory Road in 1914, where he sold Raleigh bicycles from £5 19s 6d. Alternatively he offered terms from 9s 4d a month.

An unnamed Warwick cyclist was travelling down Priory Road early in 1915 when he met a soldier riding a horse up the road, who was encouraging his animal with a whip. All three of them collided, ending up with the horse sitting on the bicycle and breaking its lamp.

With increased restrictions on travel, the use of bicycles grew, as did their riders coming into conflict with the police. During the war period, some 100 cyclists were fined for riding without lights. Not all court appearances were reported in the *Advertiser*. A traffic census held in the Coventry Road on Good Friday and Easter Monday in 1914 recorded 14,136 vehicles, of which 8,388 were bicycles.

J.B. Haddon from Birmingham unsuccessfully sued local farmer A. Jacks in 1916 for damaging his motorcycle. Haddon rode up Smith Street with a lady pillion passenger and collided with Jacks on his tractor at Eastgate. The court blamed Haddon for riding too fast.

Motor Cars
Before August 1914, Midland Autocar on the Birmingham Road sold two-seater Fords for £125, four-seater Fords for £135 and landaulettes (or town cars) for £180. By October, two-seaters had been reduced to £115 and landaulettes were now £175. In 1905 a gallon of petrol cost 7d. By 1914 this had risen to 1s 9d a gallon.

When more than 700 men from the RWR left Warwick in September, many of them were taken to Milverton railway station at Leamington by motor cars. A plea followed for more cars to be made available in future and for moving wounded soldiers around.

The military soon realized that there was a great need for motor vehicles. Advertisements appeared seeking drivers for cars and petrol lorries to join the Mechanical Transport Army Service Corps. The postings were for the duration of the war. Volunteers received 6s a day and a separation allowance if they were married. Interviews were held in Coventry and applicants could obtain a travel warrant from WBC. Three men volunteered from Warwick.

In mid-August Lord Leigh even pleaded with car owners to use less petrol, especially when they went on holiday! During the year General Quayle-Jones was driving in Myton Road when he suffered a burst tyre. He was not hurt. However, Lance Corporal Stevens of the WY was not so lucky. While driving his motorcycle in Coventry Road, he collided with a car and was 'seriously injured'.

It was not a good year for the military. Colonel Rowland John Beech, WY, appeared in court in late December. He was fined 2s plus 8s costs for driving his car without lights and declining to stop for a police constable. A.B. Wylie took advantage of the opportunities offered by new legislation and sold tail/rear lights for vehicles at 3s each.

Early in 1917, no new vehicle licences were issued; only old ones were renewed. Motor vehicle use ultimately became more restricted with petrol rationing based on a trade and not a geographical basis. More restrictions followed. Milk could only be delivered once a day.

A.B. Wylie (on the right), Warwick. (Author's collection)

Local deliveries by horse or motor vehicles were restricted to the immediate locality. Customers had to use suppliers in their own area wherever possible. Food deliveries were a priority.

The *Advertiser* approved: 'These restrictions now in force will have the effect of discouraging the practice of joyriding. There has been a great deal too much of it this year.' Joyriding in this period was not the same problem that it can be today in some areas. Early twentieth-century joyriding was just that: riding around for pleasure and wasting fuel.

As a coroner discovered, the rules were regularly enforced. He had been stopped for having his headlights uncovered during the blackout, then it was discovered that he was using his car for private purposes. Warwick magistrates fined him £2 on each count. Four cases of non-compliance with the petrol restrictions were dismissed by the same magistrates because there was no other way in which the defendants could have made these particular journeys. Car-sharing was encouraged. Yet when Brigadier General E.A. Grove was charged with using his car for an unspecified purpose, the summons was withdrawn on the instructions of the deputy chief constable. He maintained that this offence could only be dealt with by the military. There does not appear to be any record of the outcome of the case!

As the war moved into its final stages, Warwickians were urged to walk whenever possible and not to use a taxi. Motor spirit restrictions were abolished in mid-January 1919.

Trams

Trams running between Warwick and Leamington and other parts of the country faced an ever-increasing shortage of manpower. Glasgow announced in April 1915 that it was employing women as conductresses on its trams. Other towns and cities followed suit. Cynics argued that this decision was responsible for Warwick's tram crash.

In January 1916, a tram was stationary outside the Warwick Arms without its driver. The conductress mistakenly thought he was on board and released the brake. It was only as the tram gathered speed going down Jury Street that she realized her mistake. Unable to negotiate the Eastgate Arch, the tram came off its rails and crashed into the Castle Arms. Here it demolished two walls, overturned the bar counter and damaged other items such as chairs, china and pictures. Luckily only three passengers were slightly injured. Only a few days later, there was a collision between a tram and a Hunt Edmunds brewery wagon. Fortunately there were no injuries.

Electric tram on Jury Street at Eastgate, Warwick. (Author's collection)

Warwick Arms Hotel. (Author's collection)

Tram crash in Warwick, 1916. (Author's collection)

Sadly, the evening of Boxing Day witnessed a fatal collision between a tram and Annie Maria Barwell aged 55 from Leamington. Annie was described as 'being intoxicated' when she went into the Portobello Inn, long since demolished. The inn's policy was not to serve women, which was aggravated by recent legislation forbidding 'treating anyone to a drink', including one's wife. Unable to stay in the Portobello Inn, Annie left, intending to catch a tram into Leamington. Tragically, it was a foggy night and the driver did not see her wavering in the road as she tried to flag him down. His tram hit and killed her. At the inquest, the coroner

Hunt Edmunds Brewery sign. (Author's collection)

recorded a verdict of accidental death and completely exonerated the tram driver. The *Advertiser* refused to publish a letter about the incident because the sender had declined to include a name and address.

In August 1917 Mrs Toney and Mr Glover were in Emscote Road, on the Warwick side of the canal bridge, when a tram trolley came off its overhead wire and injured them. A few weeks later, the tram company successfully defended a claim for damages from Mrs

Comic tram, Warwick. (Author's collection)

Smith Street, Warwick. (Author's collection)

Hopkins of Charles Street. She claimed £8 damages sustained while alighting from the tram at Bridge Street. They proved that she had been getting off the tram before it had stopped.

On the lighter side of things, a local comedian drew what he thought about the local trams.

Motor Buses

WBC had other problems when the new motor omnibuses appeared on the scene and linked Warwick with Birmingham, Solihull, Knowle and Leamington, and stopped in the Square. The problem was on the Leamington side of the town, where the buses drove up Smith Street, competing with the trams driving down. Pleas from the town clerk for them to use St Nicholas Church Street and Castle Hill fell on deaf ears.

Note:

Travel to France was still possible in 1915, subject to certain conditions, details of which were available from the town clerk. In November of the same year, Cunard refused to take bookings from men of military age.

CHAPTER 8

Reports from the Front and Elsewhere

Letters from home were welcome, provided they contained good news. Likewise, those back home wanted personal letters and not the dreaded notification of their loved ones either being 'killed in action' or 'missing'. Yet with 'missing' notifications, there was always hope, sometimes rewarded with the good news that their missing loved one had been found.

Sometimes notices appeared in the *Advertiser* seeking news of a missing loved one, such as Major Dudley Alex Lacey Day of RWR, who had disappeared only four days after arriving in France. He was later traced to a PoW camp in Germany. In time he was promoted to the rank of colonel.

As time passed, the troops resented the total lack of appreciation back home of just how bad their living and fighting conditions really were. Censorship was rife, both at home and in the army. Officers were instructed to read the mail sent out by their men and censor it as necessary. Many did so, but not all. It was really self-censorship because the troops knew that their mail might be read by others.

DORA gave the government sweeping powers regarding the media, although generally speaking they were very anti-German and gladly suppressed any bad news that would benefit the Kaiser. The media happily published letters from men in the trenches and elsewhere that were passed on to them. In September 1914 an RWR soldier wrote that it was 'great weather and each man carried 100 rounds of ammunition', which with all their extra equipment meant an average weight of 64lb. 'Route marches of 11 miles were accomplished in 3¾ hours.' By December the 'great weather' had gone and it was now described as 'terrible'.

Following the retreat from Mons in 1914, a Warwick soldier described having to abandon their more seriously wounded when the Germans burned the village they were defending. He escaped on a spare horse and was fed by some local women. His prized possession was a piece of a shell that had landed just 30 yards from where he was sheltering. Another writer describing the same fighting wrote: 'It was a wonder our comparatively small force was not totally annihilated.' Had this letter escaped the censor or was it published as a morale-booster, showing that men survived whatever the enemy threw at them?

Even being stationed in Essex was no guarantee of safety, as Private William Gurney of the RWR wrote: 'We had a little excitement last night, which you will have read about in the papers. About 8.30pm we were visited by a hostile aircraft. The first we knew of it, was the like I have never heard before.'

In October 1914 Miss Gertrude Mann, daughter of Warwick Alderman Mann, returned from Berlin. She described the Germans as being 'gullible and believing everything they were told about the Allies being defeated'. On a lighter note, Mrs J. Sidwell at Nuneaton received an unsigned postcard from Warwick in 1915: 'Am going on alright got me clothes when I got here. Don't write [as] we have to go away. With love. PS. will send address when we get to w[h]ere we going.' Undoubtedly the writer was a soldier in transit.

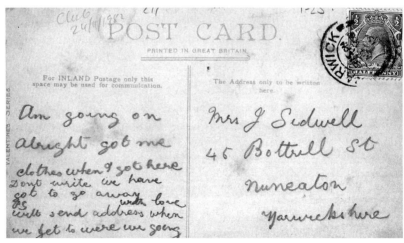

Postcard from billeted soldier. (Author's collection)

Warwick prison warder Mr Gumbley received a letter from one of his five soldier sons in March 1915: 'We were greeted early on the morning of the 21st [February] by a shell hissing through the top of our barn. We made a dash for the door, and only one fellow got hit, a spare tile hitting him on the forehead, but not seriously.' Another local man wrote a few days later:

> I crawled back about fifty yards and got hung up on some barbed wire, so that I could neither move one way or the other. I should probably have been caught like a rat in a trap had I not noticed one of our wounded travelling back. He helped me out of my tight corner.

Harry Jeffs received a letter from his son:

> After about fifteen hours of this, the Germans started using their devilish poison gas and the French had to retire and consequently us, as it is impossible to withstand the suffocating fumes… No words can describe the fiendishness of the Germans who have shelled ambulances and hospitals alike and have bayoneted our wounded as they are crawling away.

His letter was just what was needed to promote anti-German feelings. The *Advertiser* reported: 'Despite a heavy hammering, the Warwickshires reached to within seventy yards of the German trenches, but were unable ultimately to hold the position.'

Sergeant Hobbis from Swan Street wrote:

> I have been enjoying my life as a sniper for these last weeks. I started with fourteen men and a corporal, but I am sorry to say I have lost a few. Four in exchange for our bullets. We got some German shells called whizz-bangs, which are not very pleasant. [Whizz-bangs were mixed shrapnel and high-explosive shells.]

The mayor's daughter was in Dublin at the time of the Easter Rising. She was unharmed but complained about the trams not running and having to walk the 9 miles home.

Reporting generally during the Battle of the Somme was very sparse

Royal Warwickshire soldiers resting. (Public domain)

and usually confined to how well the army was doing, which was not always true. This poignant letter was written to his parents by Second Lieutenant F.B. Kay, RWR, just before going into action: 'If you receive this letter, you will know I have been bowled out middle peg. However, you may be sure I batted well.'

To avoid wholesale destruction of families and communities, recruits were now being posted to various regiments rather than just their local ones. Private G.H. Barnett, Square, serving in the 1/Northamptonshires, wrote about being shelled when on patrol: 'My mate got hit in the thigh part of his leg, and he could not get along. So I lay down and bandaged him up, and carried him safely into our own trench… The chap is in England now, but I'm sorry to tell you he lost his leg.' On 2 September 1916, the *Advertiser* wrote: 'Progress on the Western Front may be described as slow and sure. It is not sufficiently realised that we have a very big task in front of us and it will require time and patience to make much headway.'

By late 1917, tales abounded about German snipers hiding in wreckage: 'It was a sergeant of the RWR who saw him first and just in time. The German had his rifle raised at 10 yards range, but the sergeant whipped round and shot him before he could turn.'

Not all tales came from the military. Miss Dawson left the Warwick Dispensary to help nurse wounded troops at the front and ended up as sister in charge of the Acute Surgical Division at the Royal Hospital, Netley, Hampshire. The first casualty station she worked at was bombed and she wrote about some of her experiences on the front:

> Life for a nurse was one gigantic struggle… During the retreat from the Germans we were minus all our belongings, working when and where we could and having to deal with overwhelming numbers of wounded men… Amiens was one gigantic casualty clearing station…our train windows were smashed and some staff were killed by falling bombs…nights in trenches and days paddling in mud from tent to tent.

Her efforts were appreciated and she was Mentioned in Despatches. In 1917 she was awarded the Red Cross Medal by King George V.

Reports were sometimes published regarding life in Germany, such as their people being rationed to 10oz of bread per person.

CHAPTER 9

Prisoners of War

The way in which many British PoWs were treated has long remained controversial. While some of the tales could have been part of anti-German propaganda, others were certainly true. With the callous German disregard of human life, reports of ill-treatment of PoWs came as no surprise to people back home. By comparison, German PoWs in Britain had a much better time. It should not be forgotten that food and other goods were in short supply in both countries.

Repatriation schemes happened whereby corresponding numbers of prisoners from both sides were exchanged. Usually they involved PoWs who had been so seriously wounded that they would never be fit enough to fight again. An exchange planned for late October 1918 was cancelled after Germany imposed 'impossible' conditions. A previous exchange had occurred in February 1915 that included four soldiers from the RWR. However, whenever these exchanges happened, U-boat crews were specifically excluded.

German PoWs
The suggestion to use German PoWs to help on the farms, especially at harvest time, was made in early June 1915. The idea initially fell on deaf ears because the military always took precedence, regardless of the ever-growing demand for more food but with fewer workers to provide it.

Now PoWs worked on the land for 4s a day, funded by the farmers. The government agreed to pay for their food. Ideally they should all be housed in one large building, with an escort provided by the Home Defence Corps. Warwick farmers totally opposed the idea. The local opposition was ignored and possible sites around Warwick were examined with a view to building a PoW camp, mainly for men to help on the farms. However, this idea was short-lived.

By mid-1918, Warwickshire had been particularly badly hit by the conscription of agricultural workers and now had just one farm labourer for every 650 acres. Farmers were desperate for workers and had to accept help from PoWs and women. Yet they worked well and more and more of them were used. Nevertheless, the underlying opinion was that the PoWs should supplement the existing labour rather than replace it.

Although PoWs had a considerable degree of freedom, they were prohibited from buying extra food to supplement their official diet. In late August Arthur White and Robert Shellard were fined £40 and £5 respectively for selling bread to PoWs in Warwick. Their action was described 'as being likely to interfere with the discipline or administration of a place of detention of prisoners of war'. They were lucky. Weeks later a baker in nearby Solihull went to prison for three months with hard labour for the same offence.

Perhaps the integration of PoWs and women onto the land worked too well. Not long before the Armistice, farmers were instructed that PoWs were not allowed to work on the same part of the farm where women were billeted.

Within days of the Armistice, this notice appeared in the *Advertiser*: 'The Attorney General stated that it is the declared policy of the government to send back to Germany every BOCHE in the country.' [The word 'boche' comes from the French 'caboche', the dialectical meaning being 'cabbage' or 'blockhead'.] There were still PoWs around in March 1919 and farmers paid them the same rate as fixed by the wages board.

British PoWs

By early November 1914, there were 34,907 men and 417 officers captive in Germany. Among them was Major and Mrs Airth Richardson's son-in-law. He wrote to them saying that he was well-treated, playing lots of football and enjoying hot showers twice a week. However, not all PoWs were treated so well and depended on parcels from their loved ones. All enquiries about PoWs were directed to Le Bureau de la Croix Rouge Internationale in Geneva.

Civilians were also interned, as the mayor's nephew discovered. He came from Queensland and by early 1915 was interned in Berlin. Mr J. Harris from Sydney Terrace, The Cape, Warwick received a letter from his PoW son asking for food parcels of butter, chocolate powder and other eatables. The letter added that they were allowed to smoke.

As April ended, British PoWs were reported as not getting enough to eat. These reports were accompanied by tales of Germans bayoneting wounded soldiers and not taking them prisoner. The more these tales circulated, the more the anti-German feelings grew. Kitchener described them as being similar to 'the actions of the dervishes in the Sudan'. Winston Churchill also condemned them.

Also in April the *Advertiser* reported that fourteen officers and 320 other ranks from the RWR were PoWs in Germany. The same article asked for names and addresses of people who would be prepared to send parcels to them. Later the *Advertiser* published a letter from Private S. Gough, 2/RWR, pleading for food, cigarettes and underwear. He maintained that he had no friends or family who could help him. The same issue contained a letter from Private Reading, 1/RWR, thanking the mayoress for her parcels. They had taken twelve days to get to him, meaning that the bread was of a similar age!

Food parcels and their contents had to be officially approved. No more than two could be sent at any one time and they had to be made of cardboard or wood. No tinned foods were permitted and nothing could be packed in tins. When parcels were reported as not having been received, 'non-compliance with the requirements' was the standard excuse.

The children at nearby Wroxall raised £5 for parcels for RWR PoWs in Germany, which they achieved by forgoing their annual outing. The *Advertiser* wrongly reported these as coming from St Mary's in Warwick and later printed an apology. The Post Office (PO) allowed letters and money orders to be sent free of charge to PoWs in Germany but not to those held captive in Turkey.

German propaganda statements were made to PoWs alleging that Calais had fallen and 172,000 prisoners had been taken; London was being attacked by sea and by air; Scotland was in open rebellion; 42 warships had been sunk in Portsmouth; and a recent zeppelin raid on London had killed over 8,000 people.

With the onset of autumn Lord Craven, Lord Lieutenant of

Warwickshire, co-ordinated the collection of winter comforters for RWR PoWs. American reports criticizing conditions in some of the camps now appeared. The camp at Wittenberg was particularly criticized for its use of ferocious dogs and the lack of coats for prisoners. As 1916 dawned, 520 RWR PoWs were recorded.

When Private R.A. Biddle, 1/RWR, arrived back in Warwick after being exchanged, he spoke to the *Advertiser*. He had been captured during the previous May at Loos, where he lost the use of his right arm to an explosive bullet. His captors were considerate and gave him coffee and rum, but in his camp the PoWs received 6oz of black bread, a little thin soup and some coffee daily. Conditions were described as 'miserable' and he had to work. PoWs were regularly kicked by German officers. After being exchanged in the previous year, he praised the great kindness he had received in Holland. On returning to England he spent three-and-a-half months in hospital before being classed as 'medically unfit for further service'. His report ended by advising people in England not to believe the 'fairy tales' they read in the papers about the 'kindly Germans'. The ill-treatment continued and so did the parcels.

By May 1916, 25,000 parcels per week were being sent to PoWs from Britain. To be fair, the RWR not only looked after its own PoWs but also men from other regiments. Many financial collections were overseen by the deputy mayoress. Mrs Grant Duff at the British Legation in Berne arranged for bread to be sent to the PoWs at 4s a month.

One of the most amazing incidents was a postcard sent by a Warwick man to his family. He signed it 'W E R Starving', which fooled the German censor who thought it was the name of an Englishman. It told his family what the conditions were really like in his camp and they sent him food. In August, the Warwick Territorial Force Association at 46 High Street collated details of all Warwick PoWs.

Before the year was over there were more restrictions on parcels, which had to include the name and address of the sender. Fruit, perishable articles, 'pudding basins and the like' were now prohibited. Any parcels containing such items would be returned. Later it was agreed that next of kin could send parcels to their loved ones every three months, but they had to receive a coupon from the regimental 'Authorised Association' for packing parcels.

German PoW mail-censoring. (No known copyright)

WHAT TO SEND TO GERMANY

Readers of "THE WAR BUDGET" who have relatives or friends in any of the German (or Holland, etc.,) detention camps, can send parcels direct through the Post free of all charges.

Parcels should be addressed as follows:

Name (in full) ....
Rank and Regiment ....
British Prisoner of War detained in Germany (or Holland, etc.),
c/o General Post Office,
Mount Pleasant, London.

N.B. - In the case of Civilian Prisoners of War, the place of detention should be shown in the address.

Parcels may be handed in at any Post Office in the ordinary way.

From messages received from prisoners of war, we learn that many lack even the actual necessities of life, and the people at home render a national service by opening their purses and sending parcels of comforts to the brave officers and men who are suffering dire privation in the hands of the enemy.

What to send. (Author's collection)

In March 1917, it was rumoured that the Germans were employing PoWs just behind their front lines to discourage allied shelling. By December the cost of sending food and bread to Warwick PoWs cost £600 a year, or £2 7s per PoW. By February the fund had reached £582 4s 7d.

While Warwickshire men were well catered for, it was not always the case elsewhere. In April, the Royal Berkshire Regiment appealed to all Warwickian dog-lovers to contribute 2s 6d to their PoW fund.

Any doubts that Warwick people might have had regarding how their PoWs were treated were dispelled in late June 1918. After being kept in Switzerland since December 1916, Frank Warner from the King's Royal Rifle Corps returned to Guy Street to a great welcome. Having been captured in December 1914, he had endured a terrible time in Germany under a brutal regime. The prisoners almost had to fight for food, which was 3oz of black bread and half a pint of soup three times a day. They were hit by the guards if they tried to get any more. Many would not have survived if it had not been for the parcels they occasionally received from home and the motley collection of clothes they acquired.

On arrival at the camp, they were all housed in a great tent and slept on straw. Later they were forced to build their own camp, which was overrun with rats and other vermin. Until mid-July 1915, the sentries seized every opportunity to bully them. For example, any prisoner believed to have laughed at a guard would be tied to a post for three hours and pricked with bayonets. Matters improved when the bullying guards were replaced with wounded troops from the front. After they took over, parcels were received on a more regular basis.

There was great anger back in England when these tales became public knowledge, not that that made any difference to the Germans. Once Frank was considered to be no longer physically fit, he was moved to Switzerland which he described as 'just like being sent to heaven… We felt like birds out of a cage.' He and other PoWs were looked after by the YMCA until their repatriation. Frank also reported how one German village had no men left in it who were under 70 years of age. The others were all at the front.

The Lord Lieutenant suggested in 1917 that a Warwickshire Fund should be set up to cope with the PoWs' demands that would be made during the forthcoming twelve months. The RWR was especially interested.

Within a few days of the Armistice, PoWs came home in their thousands and were welcomed not only by the king but also by ordinary people. When Corporal Herbert Worrall returned, he wrote to his father who was a brother at the Lord Leycester Hospital: 'The one thing the

Germans could not understand about us was that we would laugh and keep our spirits up somehow.' Herbert was captured in the first few days of the war and had escaped three times. Once he was captured within sight of the Dutch frontier. He added about his repatriation: 'I can tell you that when I landed, tears as big as sixpences rolled down my face. The reception the people gave us was enough to make a strong man cry.'

Sergeant Davies, RWR, of 16 Bowling Green Street who was captured in October 1914 said: 'The treatment of prisoners was so bad that they must have starved if they had not received parcels from home.' Without the regular sending of food parcels, it is debatable just how many PoWs would have survived.

Corporal James Edwards related how the commandant of his PoW camp always addressed the prisoners: 'Englishmen…I hate you.' He ordered the prisoners to sleep in the open, even in winter. James's breakfast consisted of acorn/burnt barley coffee and black bread. Lunch was swede soup. Only coffee was available in the evening.

Following a visit by American observers, the non-commissioned officers (NCOs) were instructed not to work. In spite of this, the Germans tried to force them to do so but without success. The prisoners dug an escape tunnel but were prevented from using it.

To end on a happy note, Mr and Mrs Daulman of Coten End heard that their son, Trooper Harry Daulman, WY, had been killed in action in 1914. Although his family had mourned the loss of a husband and son, they never gave up hope. Then in 1916 they heard that he was a PoW of the Turks and he returned home in 1919.

CHAPTER 10

The Wounded

Casualties Abroad

In 1914 the British army was better equipped to deal with the wounded than in previous years, but nobody knew just how big a problem it would become. Florence Nightingale had forced the military medics to accept women as nurses, albeit unwillingly, in war zones during the Crimean War. Now help from the nurses would be invaluable during the coming years. Yet censorship was rife: the real numbers of casualties were not always made public at the time and homebound mail from servicemen was also subjected to the censor as previously mentioned.

Ambulances

The first few ambulance trains passing through Warwick were reported in the *Advertiser* but they soon ceased. Eagle Engineering of Warwick announced in September that they were to supply twenty railway ambulance wagons and 1,000 wheels by the end of March 1915. In December, Mr C.H. Barker from Myton Grove joined a group led by Lord Leigh of Stoneleigh for work at the front. They used his lordship's car for conveying the wounded wherever they were needed.

In January 1915, Miss Olive Chesshyre Molyneux from Leamington wanted to raise £400 to add another vehicle to Lady Bushman's Ambulance Fleet. She wanted donations from every woman named Olive. If insufficient money was raised, all donations would go to Lord Rothschild's fund for ambulance expenses.

When wounded men were due to arrive at Warwick railway station in February 1915, a reader appealed in the *Advertiser* for cars to convey

Reality of wounded soldier. (Author's collection)

them to Budbrooke Barracks. The editor advised him to approach the Red Cross.

Romantic view of wounded soldier. (Author's collection)

Casualties

The first casualty notice containing full details of killed, wounded and missing members of the RWR was published in September 1914. These notices were only the first and they soon grew longer. Sometimes no notices were published, usually when the war was not going well for the allies. However, not all deaths were caused by enemy action. Private J.G. Smith from the Castle Arms died in June 1917 from sunstroke while on board a troopship.

A few letters from commanding officers were given to the press to print. Private C.M. Pease from Emscote Road was killed by a sniper in 1917. His officer wrote: 'The only consolation I can offer you is that he very gallantly played his part in the show, and that he died instantaneously.'

ENGINEERING IN WARWICK

AN EAGLE PRODUCT ENTERING BUCKINGHAM PALACE

THE EAGLE ENGINEERING C? L?

THE EAGLE ENGINEERING COMPANY LTD.

is one of the oldest and largest Firms in the Town. They have a World wide reputation for their Municipal and Transport products. It is interesting to note that in an old Town like Warwick, Municipal Vehicles are made for cleaning the streets of many of the principal Capitals throughout the World. Their Trailers for Transport are unequalled. Another extensive branch of this Company's business is their Wireless Dept. They manufacture a large range of Sets, known as " Chakophone " and " Eagle Component Parts."

Their London Offices are situated at

44 and 45 PALL MALL

Eagle Works advert post-1918. (Author's collection)

Ford Model T ambulance, circa 1916. (Wyrdlight.com)

Such letters were not restricted to the army. Lieutenant G.J. Blackwell from Warwick was serving in the Royal Flying Corps after four years in the WY when he was killed in the same year. His officer wrote: 'He was acting as observation officer when he received the wounds from which he died. His pilot was unconscious and he tried to land the machine.'

The casualty lists reported Warwick soldiers who were killed, wounded or missing, often with very sparse details. Sometimes updates on wounded men followed. Alongside some of the casualty lists, with no apparent feelings for the bereaved families, details of new promotions were added. This was far from tactful as many of these would have resulted from the casualties.

Soldiers who were killed in action were not restricted to the ordinary townsfolk. Before 1914 came to an end, Second Lieutenant Brabazon Campbell was killed. He was the son of the town clerk. Later Councillor A.E. Smith, Alderman Mann and Sir Edward and Lady Nelson also lost sons.

Casualties Back Home

After initial treatment for their wounds, the more seriously wounded servicemen were sent back to England or well away from the fighting, if that was possible. Seriously wounded soldiers were more than happy to be taken home to recover and nicknamed their injuries as 'Blighty Wounds', meaning that they were serious enough to be treated back in Britain.

Wounded soldiers remained subject to military discipline. They wore a special poor-quality uniform of a single-breasted blue jacket with a white lining worn open at the neck, blue trousers, white shirt and red tie, plus their own cap and regimental badge. Soldiers had to salute officers at all times except after sunset. Those sitting in an omnibus had to stand and then salute.

The sudden arrival of tens of thousands of wounded servicemen caused a massive logistical problem back home, far beyond anyone's experience. The few existing hospitals were quickly overrun and alternative venues had to be found. Britain rose to the challenge and created temporary hospitals all over the country. Many of these were large country houses whose owners made them available for the duration of the war.

Physically injured servicemen were easier to assess than those suffering from neurasthenia, more commonly known as shellshock. The latter name implies that shells played a part in the condition, which was not necessarily correct. Neurasthenia is best described as the nervous system not working properly, thereby making it a mental disorder which the military did not want to accept but in time they were obliged to do so. Nevertheless, they were always on the lookout for malingerers. Generally speaking, only 1:8 sufferers were officers and they received better treatment.

A national advertisement appeared in 1919 asking for owners of country houses who were prepared to care for servicemen who were suffering from neurasthenia (nowadays known as chronic fatigue syndrome). They were paid £1 5s a week. In 1927, there were 65,000 patients still in hospital suffering from this condition.

Initially Warwickshire started with 180 beds, growing to 2,010 by the end of the war, and catered for 35,248 sick and wounded troops. These hospitals were overseen by the Red Cross. Wounded soldiers were made very welcome in Warwick. Sadly, it was a very different story during the Second World War, when Chief Constable Commander Edward Richard Busk Kemble banned servicemen from the streets if they were wearing hospital uniform.

Hospitals
Budbrooke Barracks
While being home to the RWR, the barracks also had hospital facilities for sixteen patients and six staff. Later, they had 100 beds and made regular pleas for comforts and other support from the community. Doris Hamnett, a 12-year-old schoolgirl from Saltisford, officially took a half-day off school every week so that she could shave the soldiers in the hospital. In 1915 each patient received two presents for Christmas.

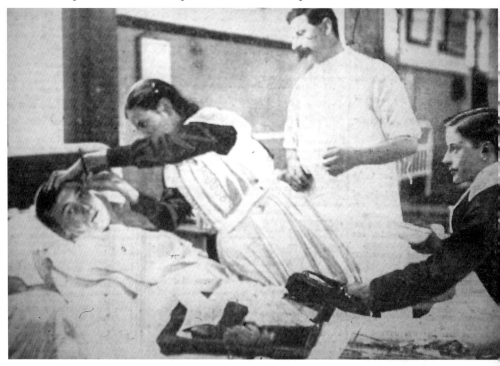

Shaving a wounded patient. (Author's collection)

Guy's Cliffe
Situated just outside Warwick, today's ruin is a far cry from the grand house that stood there in the early twentieth century. Only days after

Guy's Cliffe House, Warwick. (Author's collection)

the war started, Guy's Cliffe became a temporary hospital and soon had twenty beds.

Like so many other wartime activities, these hospitals relied heavily on charity. Appeals were made regularly for fresh vegetables, other food and reclining chairs plus fishing rods and tackle as the property's land runs down to the River Avon. Food was always gratefully received, and so were blankets when the weather grew colder.

Entrance to Guy's Cliffe, Warwick. (Author's collection)

Heathcote Isolation Hospital

Heathcote is situated just outside Warwick and had already appealed for gifts for the lonely soldiers who had to be kept in isolation. It was suggested early in 1915 that its facilities could be used for sterilizing wounds and uniforms. An approach was made to the hospital which was not answered by the matron because she was ill at the time. The cook dealt with the enquiry but she declined to answer it. Back in Warwick, the idea was shelved and the workhouse was used instead.

Hill House

Hill House has long since been demolished but in July 1915 it was turned into a Red Cross hospital with Jessie Campbell as its commandant, aided by a committee of local ladies, and £130 was collected for the project. The Congregational School in Brook Street donated 'a large basket of eggs and flowers' just before the first patients arrived. By October the facilities had increased and more equipment was needed. Girls came from the Welcome Club to help with the patients. A plea was made for the loan of sewing machines!

Funding and support from Warwickians figured very much in all these temporary hospitals and this one was no exception. In August

Hill House, Warwick. (Author's collection)

there were twenty-one patients in residence, which quickly doubled. Local auctioneer John Margetts held a sale and gave them the profits, and other organizations followed suit. The patients also helped by selling items that they had made such as rugs, baskets and nursery pictures.

Entertainment for patients included going to outside concerts, sports days, teas or places such as Warwick Castle. Some visitors received a signed photograph of the Countess of Warwick. For the less mobile, similar entertainments were provided at the hospital, often by locals. However, not everything went according to plan. The Christmas Eve play for 1915 was cancelled because the author, who was a patient, was taken ill. Christmas Day began with carol-singing at 7.00 am. The wards were decorated and the food supplemented with Christmas cake, fruit and crackers. Father Christmas visited later in the day and gave presents to everyone.

A year after opening they had sixty beds and more helpers were needed. It was a stressful time and soon afterwards the commandant, Mrs J.H. Gibbon, was ordered to rest for one month. By mid-1917, open-air wards were used when the weather permitted. These were aimed at reducing the risk of infection and promoting healing.

In early 1919, although the peace treaty had not yet been signed, everyone considered that the war was over and many temporary hospitals were returned to their owners. The management asked people who had loaned furniture and clothing etc. when it opened to arrange for their return 'wherever possible'. Hill House officially closed in March 1919.

Having opened with just 21 beds, this number peaked at 120 and had accommodated 1,717 patients, carried out 104 operations and lost only 1 patient. Commandant Miss Walker thanked her staff and all the help and support the hospital had received from the town. The closure was celebrated with a big fancy dress dinner and whist drive at the County Hall, at which event speeches were forbidden!

Longbridge Manor

The home of Airth Richardson was another temporary hospital overseen by the Red Cross. Initially it housed twelve patients, although the five wards were designed to hold twenty. These wards were described as 'having radiators, lovely views and were well supplied'.

The War Office only paid hospitals 2s per patient per day, so the hospital was always grateful for the usual gifts of food, and also for rabbits to help swell the menu.

Warwick Dispensary

This building in Castle Street also housed the cottage hospital and offered what help it could. By early 1917 it needed more money. A street collection in May the same year provided £9 9s, but a year later the dispensary owed £88, £10 more than in the previous year.

Workhouse Infirmary

This became a military hospital in September 1914, with twenty-five beds managed by the Red Cross in 1916.

Note:

The end of the war did not mean the end of wounded soldiers in Warwick and entertainments for them continued.

Medical Staff

Red Cross

None of the above hospitals could have functioned without nursing staff. There were insufficient regular nurses for this type of work and tens of thousands of volunteers were needed. In December 1914, the National Council of Trained Nurses of Great Britain and Ireland protested about the use of untrained nurses at home and abroad. What would they have preferred to do? Let the wounded soldiers die?

They and other critics of the Red Cross were quickly put in their place and their complaints were considered to be of 'small importance'. In the first six months of the war, the Red Cross nursed 19,756 patients in 705 hospitals throughout the country.

The Warwick Branch of the Red Cross quickly took over 24 Jury Street, under the jurisdiction of Brigadier General Quayle-Jones. Volunteers soon joined them and were quickly trained in basic skills. Street collections, flag days, proceeds from entertainments and sales, flower shows, etc. became regular sources of much-needed income. By 1919 they were the main recipient of such funding in Warwick.

The Red Cross helped relatives to visit seriously wounded soldiers at home and in France. They also gave medically-related talks in

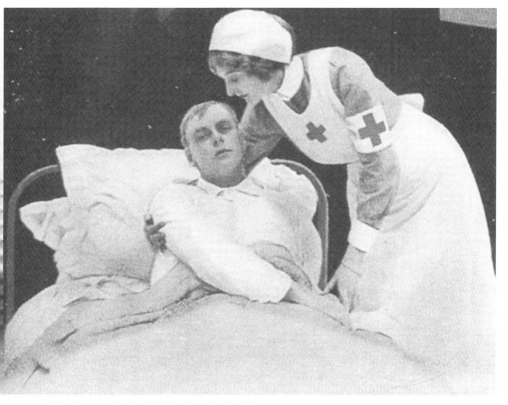

Nursing patients. (Author's collection)

Warwick, along with later advice on encouraging food production.

A route march for the Warwick Volunteer Defence Corps in early March 1915 included Red Cross stretcher-bearers. The marchers were cheered by the patients and nurses when they passed Longbridge Manor.

Ignoring all the good work carried out by the Red Cross, critics still belittled them whenever possible, such as in late 1915 when it was suggested that there were many men in the Red Cross who should be in the army. Yet just like the army, the Red Cross always needed more volunteers.

The Voluntary Aid Detachment

Known as the VAD, they provided the actual nursing staff, who wore grey cotton or white wool dresses, black woollen capes, white cotton aprons and black leather shoes.

Being a nurse was not without its risks. Janet Mary Greatorex was a sister in the Territorial Nursing Service, living at 14 Broad Street, Warwick. She came originally from Ashbourne in Derbyshire and was 38 years old when she died in 1916 of the 'Spotted Fever', another name for meningitis.

Janet Mary Greatorex on Warwick war memorial. (Author's collection)

Medical Supplies

While drugs, medicines, etc. were major essentials of any hospital, so were bandages. With more than 2,000,000 British soldiers wounded, miles and miles of bandages were needed and many of them came via Queen Mary's Needlework Guild (the Guild).

October 1916 saw the opening of the Warwick Depot at 9 & 11 Smith Street for supplying bandages to hospitals. A few days later it moved to the Priory, where fifty volunteer ladies made dressings for local hospitals. However, the Guild needed more members and more funds. During one week in May 1918, the Guild made and sent bandages, bed-jackets, shirts and 570 dressings to London in response to an urgent order during the last desperate push by the Germans.

CHAPTER 11

Health

Health in the early twentieth century was carefully monitored. WBC required reports of various diseases, some of which are considered to be fairly trivial today. It was important for WBC to know what was happening, health-wise, both in and around Warwick.

In early January 1914 there was a typhoid epidemic at nearby Kenilworth, with another one a year later. Between January and May, forty-seven cases of tuberculosis were reported in Warwick. Once the war started, local doctors treated the wives and families of servicemen without charge. With no National Health Service at that time, alternative remedies abounded. One promotion encouraged weight loss by rubbing herbs on one's body. In January 1915, Dr Saleeby MD FRS lectured on the benefits of inoculation but only to members of the WY.

Smallpox in March was confined to just one case. Some schools closed in May following an outbreak of mumps. By mid-year, tuberculosis (a respiratory disease that could affect other organs) was a major problem in Warwick and was accompanied by an outbreak of scarlet fever, erysipelas (both skin diseases), and diphtheria (a membrane disease). The town clerk headed a campaign to eradicate all flies which were thought to be 'allies of the Kaiser'.

When a large military camp was held at Wedgnock in August, WBC ensured that local springs were not contaminated. WBC instructed owners of unsatisfactory wells 'to put them right'.

The December sickness-related death rate in Warwick was five times more than at nearby Stratford. The influx of Belgian troops suffering from widespread typhus was blamed. WBC refused to renew the licence for the knackers' yard at Myton until the owner ceased boiling up horseflesh.

John and Annie Lloyd-Evans of the High Street became authorized visitors to the houses registered 'for the reception of lunatics in the Borough of Warwick'. From 1 January 1917, measles and German measles became notifiable diseases. In May Emscote Infants School was closed after an outbreak of measles. Between 12 June and 27 October, a clinic held at Warwick School examined 108 children, 67 of whom suffered from skin diseases.

After 1 March, malaria (a mosquito-borne disease), dysentery, 'French fever' (venereal disease), acute primary pneumonia (inflammation of the lungs) and acute influenza became notifiable diseases. The following month, Warwick District Nursing Association provided care for the numerous cases referred to them by the Pneumonia Order for which they received £1 5s per week per patient.

Water Supply and Sewage Problems

WBC reported early in January 1914 that Warwick water was generally good and pure. However, in late June concern was raised about the unsatisfactory state of the wells at Longbridge. Six months later, they were blamed for an outbreak of diphtheria. Within the month, WBC advertised for a working engineer at the sewage pumping station. The successful candidate needed practical knowledge for a salary of £1 15s per week.

In July complaints arose regarding untreated sewage going straight into the River Avon. Although the problem was being addressed, there were no temporary facilities in place to stop the leaks. The Reverend F.H. Lawson, vicar of St Nicholas, preached a blistering sermon on the subject just a few days later. He described the pollution 'as a most un-neighbourly and unchristian act...deliberate refusal to obey the law... a town council has no more justification for doing an unchristian act than an individual has.' He was supported by local letter-writer Amos C. Mills from Cape Road.

Councillor Smith was furious at what had been said and blamed the war, wet conditions, labour problems and reliance on the railway to deliver the more essential materials. The work was completed in late September, when it was agreed that the workmen could enlist if they

St Nicholas Church, Warwick. (Author's collection)

wished but not just yet. It was a new system and they were still needed to ensure that it worked properly.

Early in 1918 WBC declined to support any request from its workforce for deferment of military service, with the exception of the Sewage Farm Manager and the Works electrical engineer. Their plans all went awry when Sewage Farm Manager J.W. Stopps, a conscientious objector, resigned in July. A new manager was needed, at a salary of £170 per annum.

Water Tower

Following a burst water main in early 1916, the old water tower in Market Street became a reserve in case of fire, provided it was thoroughly cleaned and the existing water changed. When the water was checked six months later, it was described as 'unsatisfactory'.

Venereal Disease

These were worldwide sexually transmitted diseases (STDs) and a big problem. The popular song about what a soldier brought back from France could have had quite another meaning!

'Khaki Fever.' (Author's collection)

Warneford Hospital, Leamington Spa. (Author's collection)

Prostitution and a general decline in morals were an offshoot of the war, which alarmed both the military and civil authorities. It was proposed that the police should regularly check up on the morals of wives of serving soldiers; however, the police declined to do so.

Many young women were accused of suffering from 'Khaki Fever', or being promiscuous with soldiers. The Women's Army Auxiliary Corps (WAAC) and munitionettes (female munitions workers) were accused of being particular offenders. Whatever the truth of such statements, a more prevalent source of VD came from returning soldiers after their romps with foreign prostitutes.

Only duly qualified people were authorized to treat VD. Unauthorized practitioners faced the possibility of £100 fines or six months in prison with hard labour. Warwick had no facilities for treating VD and patients needed to visit the Warneford Hospital in Leamington, on Tuesdays for females and Mondays for males. Alternatively, patients could be treated at the Birmingham General Hospital.

By March 1919 WBC was so concerned about VD that they formed a committee to deal with it, mainly by propaganda. The problem lay not just in the disease but also in the treatment. Patients failing to complete the treatment made matters worse and warning notices were published in the press to that effect.

Birmingham General Hospital. (Author's collection)

St Paul's Church, Warwick. (Author's collection)

The Reverend E.H. Longland from St Paul's would have felt much vindicated by what was happening. In March 1915 he had made a blistering attack on the antics of young women in the town:

> Complacency is the rust of efficiency…thriftlessness and drink…shameful behaviour of silly girls in the street. The price of beer has risen considerably but the amount consumed has

Warwick girls. (Author's collection)

risen. One pint a day equals £6.1s.8d a year...unseemly behaviour of women in our streets is escalating... No self-respecting man will pick his wife out of a pack of giddy un-maidenly girls in the street... Measures will have to be considered.

The Reverend moved to Droitwich later in 1915 for undisclosed reasons.

Spanish Flu
As if there were not enough deaths during the war, during its latter stages yet another killer arrived on the scene: Spanish influenza or Spanish flu as it was most often known. The virus was believed to have moved from Asia to Spain and thence into France and the rest of Europe. Spain, being a neutral country and not subject to media censorship, was the first country to admit experiencing it, hence the rather misleading name of 'Spanish flu'.

The virus, possibly a mutation of bird and swine flu, lasted for about seventy-two hours and was highly contagious. If the sufferers did not contract bronchial problems then they would most likely survive. There was no treatment for it: one either survived or died. It is uncertain just how many died, but recent research suggests as many as 50,000,000. Unusually for influenza, the 20 to 40 age group was the most susceptible (it customarily mainly strikes the very young, the elderly and those with auto-immune deficiencies). Censorship of the time ensured that newspaper reports gave it a low profile, if any.

The outbreak arrived in the trenches, where overcrowding, exhaustion and malnutrition were rife, and spread from there. Back home, as 1918 drew to a close, the flu arrived, usually following the railway routes used by returning troops.

There are no official figures for Warwick but approximately 24,000 people are believed to have died in Warwickshire. By late October 1918 the flu was spreading in Warwick, although no deaths had yet been reported. This all changed a week later when it was reported as abating in Warwick and Kenilworth and being contained, yet still causing several deaths! The following week's news recorded forty fatalities in Warwick during the last quarter of 1918. These were one of the very few sets of figures published. Other reports talked about a 'high death rate' with no actual figures.

Advice for warding off infection included the following: 'Rooms were to be flushed with fresh air. Overcrowding to be avoided as was alcoholism... Spitting was a source of infection and actively discouraged...diluted Jeyes Fluid [was suggested]...as a preventative gargle and inhalant[!]. It could also be sprinkled on clothes and bedding.'

Several school closures followed. Just before the Armistice, Warwick School proudly announced that they would re-open as no pupils or staff had the flu. The elementary schools soon followed suit.

December saw bland reports about the flu 'still showing some signs of abatement'. When a fresh outbreak was feared in the spring, King's High School took no chances and postponed their annual prize-giving until February 1919.

CHAPTER 12

Warwick at War

Note:
The following chapter may appear somewhat disconnected in terms of subject matter, but it essentially covers the effects of the war on Warwickians in roughly chronological order.

***

The war affected everyone and many families had their lives ruined forever. While the men were away fighting, life at home still went on, regardless of how difficult it might be. Nevertheless, what was happening abroad often affected those who were left behind.

After war was declared, the Royal Proclamation was read to a huge crowd of people outside the Court House. The churches had prayers said. A few days later, Canon Llewellyn Wood became the new vicar at St Mary's. The Post Office worked non-stop dealing with an 'enormous number of telegrams'. The *Advertiser* commented that in the following week, 'the town was full of soldiers.'

Many businesses soon experienced financial problems. Some goods were already in short supply, while grocers and certain other traders demanded cash with orders. Many houses suddenly cut down on domestic servants or did away with them completely.

Later in August, the Post Office only accepted telegrams destined for abroad at the sender's risk. They had to be in English or French but only in French if going to Switzerland or Turkey. Letters home from servicemen were sent free of charge. Local items posted were still delivered on the same day. They were so busy that the Boy Scouts were employed to help with the workload.

Henry H. Lacy, bookseller and stationer of 8 High Street, telephone no. 16, stocked up on maps and illustrated papers relating to the war. Mrs Smith-Ryland's committee collected spare clothing and blankets for wounded soldiers and stored them at the Pageant House. A requiem mass was held at St Mary Immaculate Roman Catholic Church for the late pope at the end of August. Sunday's sermon was a protest against the *Church Times* having referred to him as 'a knave and a simpleton'. Mayor John Lloyd-Evans agreed to stand for another year as he felt it was undesirable to change 'in the present circumstances'.

Samples of the official postcards from servicemen in France were printed showing which sentence the sender could tick: 'I am quite well: I have been admitted into hospital sick and am going on well/wounded and hope to be discharged soon. I have received your letter/telegram/ parcel: Nothing else to be written or the card would be destroyed.'

In late November A.B. Wylie of the Cornmarket announced that they had received an order from the War Office for the supply of 10,000 spurs, as they had during the Boer War. The shop also advertised a 'Choicest selection of Gifts' as Christmas approached. A 50 per cent clearance sale of trinkets, silver purses, smelling salts, etc. soon followed. The store housed a wide variety of goods, as demonstrated by an advertisement in 1915 for the sale of 'fly and maggot oil'. Leather goods came later.

As the year ended there were pleas for comforts for the troops as the war was obviously going to continue for months to come. Various committees collected gloves, pullovers, food, socks, etc. for the ill-equipped troops. Another appeal was made for mouth-organs and sandbags. Appeals were still being made late in 1917.

A War Emergency Committee (WEC) met in December. It arranged the transport of recruits to Budbrooke, organized the distribution of lemonade and food for soldiers going off to war, and formed a veteran rifle club. The WEC boasted of being the first in Britain to use military bands to help with recruiting in the previous October.

New Year's Eve saw the worst floods since 1900. As 1915 began, Warwick soon discovered that any suitable part of the town would be used for training purposes. In February Miss Ashmore, a partial invalid of 89 Emscote Road, completed her forty-ninth garment and forty-third pair of socks for the troops. In late March some 3in of snow fell. Snow also fell in May and heavy rain came in September. Despite the untold misery caused everywhere by the war, the *Advertiser* reported in early May that a cuckoo had been heard in Warwick!

The mayor attended a special service in St Mary's on the first anniversary of the war, based on a similar one in St Paul's, London. Afterwards there was a large gathering in the Square where the band from Budbrooke played the national anthems of all the allies, followed by several short speeches.

The army appealed for non-military men to clean chimneys, remove ashes, empty privies, closets, septic plots and clean latrine strainers. Thacker & Christmas Ltd, grocers at 22-24 High Street, now closed daily for lunch and other shops followed suit. Mr E.M. Pollock, the local Member of Parliament, called at Eagle Engineering for a morale-boosting visit to the workers who were involved in making war materials.

In November the mayor announced his retirement, being unable to serve for the duration of the war as he had wanted. He was succeeded by the Earl of Warwick, Francis Richard Charles Guy Greville.

Later that month, the Reverend J. Cairns of St Nicholas instructed all members of the Warwickshire Amateur Ordnance Volunteers under the command of Lord Leigh to mobilize. The aim was to use their lathes for making shell cases. Every hour of such work carried out away from munitions factories meant a quicker production rate of shells. These shell cases had a very low rejection rate. A captured German gun was publicly exhibited in Birmingham.

For the second year, drapers J. Hatton in the Square promoted military fashion, concentrating on khaki gloves, shirts, socks, etc. These were aimed at the home market to purchase for their menfolk wherever they served. A.B. Wylie advertised another 'Choicest selection of Gifts' for the forthcoming Christmas. The Post Office needed twenty temporary workers to help with the pre-Christmas rush.

J.H. Bray sold sweetheart brooches consisting of an antelope with a rifle or a bear and ragged staff. They cost 1s each plus 1d postage. For the men, at the same price plus 2d postage was a 'Soldier's Pocket Mirror' that was made of plated metal and promised 'a bullet could not penetrate…may save a valuable life.'

January 1916 was described as being the mildest on record but not

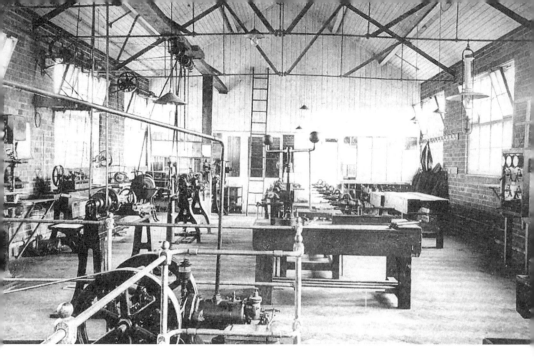

Warwick School engineering workshop. (Author's collection)

Warwick Market Place, aka the Square. (Author's collection)

the calmest of weather. A couple being married at St Nicholas Church on 2 January had a lucky escape when a pinnacle was blown down. Heavy rain later hampered the harvest, quickly followed by 'brilliant' weather that improved the crops.

The mayoress purchased a large quantity of woollen material for making into shirts for the soldiers in France. Starting on 6 March, there were only two postal deliveries daily. A Chamber committee agreed in May to look after businesses whose owners had been conscripted. There were thirty-eight businesses in Warwick affected at this time. One example was Frederick Hine, butcher in the Square. Both his sons had been conscripted and, unable to get any help, he was obliged to close his business after it had been running for thirty-two years.

A rumour spread that Warwick's Post Office would be downgraded to a sub-Post Office. While it was not confirmed, certain services were moved to Leamington in July. Following Lord Kitchener's death in June, a memorial service for him was held at St Mary's Church. Shop trading hours for the coming winter were now regulated by the police, assisted by the Chamber. They closed at 6.00 pm on Mondays and Tuesdays; 1.00 pm on Thursdays; and 8.00 pm on Fridays and Saturdays. They returned to 7.00 pm closing in March 1917.

The government proudly announced its new weapon: the tank. All soldiers in Britain were permitted to spend Christmas with their families after a previous order was rescinded in the face of public opinion. In February 1917 Charles Savage Landor aged 91, the sole surviving son of Walter Savage Landor, had died in Florence. His father was one of the more scandalous residents of Warwick, whose hobby was insulting people.

A hailstorm in mid-June was described as being 'of a size never seen before'. The Dodd & Wilson hairdresser and tobacconist partnership was dissolved in July. Arthur Randall Dodd could not continue in business on his own once his partner James Wilson had been conscripted.

Soldiers were given a pay rise in September from 3s to 3s 6d per day, which would cost an extra £130,000,000 per year. Later a big military service held in the Square, which was attended by troops stationed in and around Warwick with scouts and voluntary groups, etc. raised £13 0s 8d for the Red Cross.

Airth Richardson struggled to cope with his military and mayoral duties. He was probably relieved to be suddenly recalled to duty. Someone wrote to the *Advertiser* complaining about public clocks in Warwick all telling different times. A similar complaint had been made in 1820! In November, the Avon Foundry in Avon Street made munitions, although apart from the obvious explosive dangers, munitions work caused respiratory complaints and skin problems.

The pope gave special permission in November for a solemn requiem mass to be held in St Mary Immaculate for all soldiers and sailors who had been killed in the war to date. Father Murphy thanked the Warwickshire Needlework Guild for the thirty garments they had given him.

Sir Edward Montague Nelson, Knight Commander of the Order of St Michael and St George (KCMG), local businessman and politician, was appointed mayor although he was not a member of WBC. He was the successful owner of George Nelson Dale & Co. who had also lost a son, Walter, in 1915. The family had lived in the Pageant House in the earlier part of the century before selling it to WBC after the 1906 pageant. Sadly he suffered a fatal stroke in February 1919. Thanks to his efforts, £184,000 was raised for war purposes.

Sir Edward Montague Nelson.
(Warwick Visitor Centre)

When the conscription age was raised to 55 in 1918, the question was asked as to why younger munitions men were not being conscripted. Soon afterwards munitions workers went on strike in Coventry, where they were condemned for being 'selfish'. The strike soon collapsed when the government announced that if the strikers did not return to work, they would swiftly be conscripted. Other strikers were given the same ultimatum.

In late August, Alexander Brown Wylie aged 47 died from septic pneumonia, having been ill for a month. He had come to Warwick in 1890 and with Mr Harbage set up A.B. Wylie Ltd as ironmongers in Coten End. His widow took over the management of the business. By this time American visitors were welcomed in Warwick but they had to bring their ration books with them. On 1 November, the Bishop of Coventry led a service in St Mary's for Warwick servicemen who had lost their lives to date.

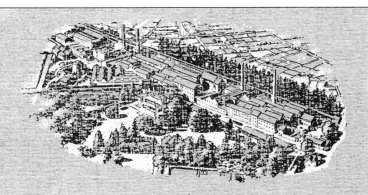

Emscote Mills, Warwick

Emscote Mills, Warwick, the home of Nelson products since 1837, are situated in beautiful rural surroundings, amidst green fields and trees and close to Leamington, the famous Spa.

At the present day the ten factories cover an area of over 5 acres and are well ventilated hygienic buildings equipped with the most up-to-date machinery.

The employees have a first rate Club building—The Nelson Club—which is a standing monument to the kindly thought and generous treatment of a firm which, even in these days of " grab and get," still maintains that " human touch " which ministers to the happiness and comfort of those who serve it.

The Castle is a monument of History, and Emscote Mills is equally a monument of Industry. It is perhaps entitled to a place in Commercial History even if only for the fact that it gave to the world that culinary delicacy—the table jelly.

Nelson's present day culinary Gelatine is their " Waferleaf," and with its aid many delightful dishes can be contrived.

Their delicious "Fruitlets" are a favourite sweetmeat and are obtainable from Automatic Machines and Confectioners throughout Great Britain and abroad.

A high grade Gelatine used by Photographic Film Manufacturers also forms an important part of the manufacturing activities of this old established House—whose wares are known throughout the civilised World.

Messrs.

GEO. NELSON DALE & Co.
LIMITED
EMSCOTE MILLS, WARWICK

Nelson Dale advert post-1918. (Author's collection)

As the year ended, DORA rescinded the early closing regulations just before Christmas and Lieutenant Colonel Airth Richardson chaired a mass meeting at Shire Hall regarding the forthcoming General Election.

American President Woodrow Wilson visited in early January 1919 and stayed at The Woolpack. By the end of January, munitions factories were returning to pre-war manufacturing. As the weeks progressed, WBC became very disenchanted with the PO and accused them of being 'prejudicial to the interests' of Warwickians. By March, the PO was opening at 8.00 am and supplied an afternoon delivery between 4 and 4.30 pm. However, only a few days later the mayor complained that his mail did not arrive until 9.50 am. 'I think we ought to do all that we can to put this matter right,' he said. The general feeling of WBC in May was that 'the post office was not interested in making changes.' Soon afterwards, the Post Office in Emscote Road was closed, although there was a promise to re-open it.

Councillor Austin Edwards became the next mayor. The Reverend B. Howard Clark disappeared in the same month. Originally from Warwick, he had moved to a parish in Leicester in 1918. He left there one morning in late February, saying that he was going to London and had not been seen since. His friends and family were worried because he had mental problems and financial difficulties. It was a forlorn hope that he might have returned to Warwick.

CHAPTER 13

Women

As the twentieth century dawned, stern Victorian attitudes remained about the role of women in society. Where women had to work, it was accepted that they were useful as maids, cooks, housekeepers, nurses, etc. but they should not seek any higher role. Some rebels defied convention and made a career for themselves but they were rare. The advent of the suffragettes changed many of these entrenched views but much more change was needed.

In the early stages of the war, women's role remained the same but with the added task of encouraging the men to go out and fight. With no immediate prospects of peace, women formed numerous committees to help the men. Some knitted comforts for them, although many of these items were not really wanted. The troops complained about how these comforts delayed the receipt of much-needed supplies.

As the war progressed, especially following conscription, there was a voracious demand for men, leaving vital jobs desperately in need of being filled. This was where women came into their own. Yet there would still be a need for the traditional female workers. In December 1914, this advertisement appeared in the *Advertiser*: 'Young gentlewoman wanted, as daily companion: foreigner preferred.'

March 1915 saw women officially being recruited for all manner of jobs. By 3.00 pm on the first day, 700 had enrolled in London, with local application forms available from the Labour Exchange in Leamington. Later in the year, 150,000 women were wanted for clerical jobs in order to release more men for military service.

A meeting was held in April at St Paul's parish room. The topic was 'What the girls can do: Pledge to do our bit. As the government was

now offering work to women, they should take advantage of it.'
Approximately 10,000 women per month enlisted in the WAAC after
its inauguration in March 1917. Its members were subject to the same
military disciplinary code, as discovered by Maud Staine. She was
fined 5s at Warwick for being absent without official leave.

There were many men who thought that once the war had ended,
women would then revert to their old roles in life. However, they were
in for a shock. For example, when 6,000 demobilized women in Leeds
were offered positions in domestic service, they all refused. A religious
paper in May 1919 blamed the fall in congregations on conscription,
munitions workers, Spanish flu and working women. The roles of local
women working in the war are covered in the appropriate chapters.

WAAC advert. (Public domain)

CHAPTER 14

Children

The war was an exciting time for many children, giving them legitimate excuses to miss school. Most of the older boys waited impatiently until they could go and fight. They were aware that their fathers and older brothers were away fighting, but that was all part of the adventure. If my experiences of growing up during the last war are anything to go by, younger children would have been unaware of what 'the war' really meant. A father was someone you might or might not see occasionally but we had no real concept of death.

Between 1914 and 1918, life at home continued as best as it could. Local education committees struggled, often unsuccessfully, to maintain some degree of normality in the schools. The official line was that nothing should interfere with schooling.

General
America sent 300 toys to Warwickshire and Belgian refugee children for Christmas 1914. They repeated this gesture to all the countries involved in the war. However, a total of 300 was nowhere near enough and caused numerous problems. The toy shortage in Warwick was eased slightly when the Misses Cullis provided twelve dolls for the children. 'Our Fight for the Empire' was the title of a Lantern Lecture that raised funds for Dr Barnardo's in mid-January 1915.

The opportunity for children to work on the land, where necessary, was recognized in February, albeit with age and distance restrictions. WCC fiercely contested the idea.

A group of Warwick ladies formed a Tipperary Club for the wives and children of servicemen in late 1914. This club operated on

Wednesday afternoons at 13 Old Square. By early January 1915, more than 80 mothers and 180 children had enrolled. After tea at the first meeting, there was a present for each child followed by a cinematograph show given by Mr and Mrs Smith-Ryland.

On 10 February, the occupants of 84 Cliffe Hill found a 14-day-old baby boy abandoned on their doorstep. He was taken to the workhouse. Later, Kate Pretty of 4 Linen Street went to prison for three months with hard labour for unlawfully abandoning her child. No reference was made about the father.

Teachers soon protested about the number of children being kept away from school for 'agricultural reasons' but this problem was not going to go away. At their April meeting Warwickshire Education Committee (EC) agreed to release children aged 11 or older for farm and market garden work. Then the committee changed its mind and only allowed boys aged 12 or older to work, and only then if older children and adults were not available. They were paid 6s per week and girls could also be considered. WCC objected to this new and confusing policy. The arguments continued unresolved into harvest time. If the WCC figures are to be believed, there were less than two children per parish so employed. After the harvest all children under 11 returned to school. Nevertheless, the EC remained unhappy.

Celebrating Empire Day on 24 May, approximately 2,000 local infant children and their teachers marched to Warwick Castle. Here they saluted the Union Jack on Guy's Tower and listened to the Earl of Warwick.

By March 1917, as the U-boat activities increased, children were allowed to work on farms but not in market gardens! The arguments soon surfaced again when women, supported by troops, were employed on the land. Why were children needed?

Legislation passed in early March required all children over 3 years of age to be removed from the 'contaminating atmosphere of the workhouse'. By early November there was a considerable rise in widows' weekly war pensions, especially for those with children. A childless widow would receive 7s 6d. With one child she would receive 12s 6d, and with four children £1 0s 6d.

As Christmas approached, Mrs Thorneycroft organized a street collection to raise funds to purchase treats for the children of serving soldiers and sailors. However, not everyone was that keen on children. In August 1918 Lady Nelson opened her gardens to the public at the site known as The Lawns (later Emscote Lawn School), on the strict understanding that children would not be admitted!

Infants

The Warwick Infant Health Society started in 1912 and two years later they expanded their work. A Babies Club opened at St Nicholas Parish Rooms every Friday from 3.00 pm to 4.00 pm. Practical demonstrations were given on baby care. Expansion plans progressed and in May 1916 the rooms became the Infant Welfare Centre.

By early 1917, larger crèche facilities were needed to look after very young children so that their mothers could go to work. When it opened in June the crèche accepted children from 6.00 am to 7.00 pm and until 2.00 pm on Saturdays. Mothers paid 8d a day, which included food for their children. Some financial help came from West Gate Auctions. In 1917 WBC highlighted a lack of children's books in the town library.

A Baby Week held in July raised £60 2s for the Warwick Day Nursery. The climax was a fête in the Castle Park with a prize for the 'best turned out perambulator'. Admission was free and other entertainment was provided by the RWR Band, and Boy Scouts danced round a maypole! In September, 1-year-old Robert Henry Wilkins won the baby show contest at the Military Sports Day.

A scheme introduced in 1918 enabled milk for children to be purchased at a reduced price. July saw more National Baby Weeks held in different parts of the town. An exhibition was held at 3 The Butts (the home of Warwick Day Nursery).

Coten End School

In early December 1914, a large consignment of comforts was sent to the 1/RWR and 2/RWR by the Mayoress Mrs Lloyd Evans. Included in the consignment was a parcel of cigarettes and chocolates provided by the pupils and staff of Coten End School. The pupils had saved their pennies for this gift. Soon after its receipt, the officer-in-charge of 1/RWR publicly thanked the children on behalf of both battalions. Not content with just one parcel, the same pupils forfeited their Christmas tea to raise more funds both for the RWR and the Belgian refugees. The school was also still used for adult education such as mechanical drawing and shorthand in late 1918.

Library at King's High School, Warwick. (Author's collection)

King's High School

As 1914 ended, the pupils contributed 14s 5½d to the Belgian Refugees Fund. Termly fees in 1915 ranged from £1 10s to £3 for girls living outside Warwick, while local pupils paid £2 to £2 10s. The boys paid £3 3s if local and £3 17s if not. In October 1916, the school governors sued Alfred Owens from Leamington for the £3 he owed in school fees. He maintained that his daughter had not attended the school because of ill health but he still had to pay.

Staff room at King's High School, Warwick. (Author's collection)

In April 1915, the Girls' School applied to the Henry VIII Charity for permission to use the Eastgate Arch. A few days later, they advertised for a 'respectable man' to act as caretaker. No salary was mentioned.

Towards the end of the year, the mayoress presented the school certificates and stressed that this is 'no age for idle and indifferent women'. On 14 and 15 December, the girls entertained disabled servicemen with a concert.

Warwick School
Sixty old boys from the school (OWs) joined the 7/RWR Territorials soon after war was declared. As the autumn term progressed, the school's army cadets could not obtain enough khaki cloth for uniforms, so they appealed for any old uniforms. Very few OWs attended the annual reunion because so many of them were serving in the forces.

The school gymnasium was used for rifle instruction in early 1915 for the Warwick Defence Corps who still needed more men. By December, the workshop manufactured munitions. At harvest time the school took part in a successful 'experiment'. Seven pupils worked several miles out of town. Free travel was provided by train or car and they earned 2s per day plus free meals. This was repeated with twenty-four pupils and a teacher going to Wiltshire. Similar schemes worked elsewhere in Britain. Termly fees in 1919 were £9 9s to £11 11s for Warwick boys and others paid £12 to £15.

Westgate School for Boys
Pupils collected 23cwt of blackberries in early October 1918 (see references to jam-making in Chapter 16).

Westgate School for Girls
Pupils raised £7 for the relief of Warwick PoWs in 1916. From mid-1917 the school was used for cookery classes in preparing economical food. By early October 1918 pupils collected 6¾cwt of blackberries and donated £25 towards the National Egg Collection Scheme for Wounded Soldiers. During this period, children from all over Warwickshire collected 30.5 tons of blackberries.

Miscellaneous Education

During the autumn of 1914, Warwick Higher Education Committee ran courses at the Art and Technical School situated in The Butts, Coten End and Westgate. The committee produced a pamphlet explaining why England was at war. The Board of Education agreed in 1915 (probably unwillingly) to introduce military drill into elementary schools. Warwick teachers protested about children leaving school before the age of 14 to work in agriculture and industry.

School attendance for April 1915 averaged 91 per cent with Westgate Boys making 97 per cent and Coten End Infants coming last with 86 per cent. It was a different story the following month when several schools closed due to an outbreak of mumps.

There was a perpetual shortage of farm labour during the year, which strengthened the demand to employ schoolboys. Early in the next year, it was felt nationally that too many children under the age of 12 were missing school for agricultural reasons. It was felt that by mid-1917, there would be enough women and troops working on the land so children would no longer be needed. However, this proved to be wishful thinking.

Teachers

In September 1914, the EC agreed to use teaching volunteers but only if WCC agreed. Teachers were no doubt dismayed to find that they were not exempt from military service. Those who appealed to local tribunals found them not very sympathetic.

A wartime bonus of 3s per week for married men and 2s per week for single men, widowers and widows was introduced by WCC in January 1917. An extra bonus of 1s per week was added for each child under the age of 14. Teachers considered these bonuses to be 'utterly inadequate'. Mechanics earned more! By May a certificated male teacher received £100 per annum and his female counterpart £90. Uncertificated teachers were paid £65.

Nothing changed and there was a shortage of teachers by mid-1918. As the end of the war approached, the local branch of the National Federation of Women's Teachers met at St Mary's Church Hall and demanded 'equal pay for equal work'.

CHAPTER 15

Warwick Castle

Throughout its long history, Warwick Castle and its earls have had a major influence on the town's history but times were not always kind to some of the earls. Such was the case in 1914 when the earl was short of funds. It was a time when many owners of these large old family mansions were feeling the pinch. Some income could be raised by opening up the building to the public but that was rather a drop in the ocean. A more reliable source of funds was to let the building, as happened here.

Castle & Park
Within hours of the outbreak of war, the chef and chauffeur returned home and joined the French army. During May 1916, the tenants were treated to a party with an organ recital and songs. The next day Mr and Mrs W.M. Hughes, the Australian premier and his wife, were guests of the earl and countess.

The castle was a regular venue for military inspections and other events. Part of the official peace celebrations in 1919 involved sports and dancing in the park, accompanied by the Wyken Brass Band.

Francis Richard Charles Guy Greville, 5th Earl of Warwick, and Frances Evelyn Maynard, aka 'Darling Daisy', Countess of Warwick
The earl introduced a bill in the House of Lords to improve the country's defences even before the war started. It was defeated by 53 to 34 votes and he was severely criticized for introducing it. However, he was more far-sighted than many of his peers and continued to

Entrance to Warwick Castle. (Author's collection)

Earl and Countess of Warwick. (Author's collection)

publicize the dangers of invasion. Practising what he preached, in his role as Lord Lieutenant of Essex he issued instructions about the action Essex people should take in the event of an invasion.

As the year drew to a close, the countess visited war hospitals in France. In early January 1915 as a colonel in the WY, the earl inspected 455 officers and men in the courtyard. He still worried about a possible invasion and hoped there would be enough volunteers to negate the need for conscription. He supported campaigns to recruit more men, stressing how 'the lack of weapons has cost us dear'.

Back in Warwick, he became mayor of the town for the third time. Almost at once he received an appeal from the Queen Mary's Convalescent Auxiliary Hospital on behalf of Private G.H. Coney from Pickard Street. He needed £40 to be fitted with a false arm. Donations of £25 had already been promised, to which he added £1. The balance was collected in town and included £1 donated by the Misses Heath at Guy's Cross Hill.

On various occasions during 1916, the countess entertained wounded servicemen from Budbrooke Barracks. If the weather was fine, they went on the river. In March 1917 the earl contributed towards the £157 6s that was raised for providing a bed for the Anglo-Russian Hospital in Petrograd. The Warwick coat of arms was attached to it.

Countess of Warwick. (Author's collection)

(The cost may seem high but this would have been a state-of-the-art medical bed including various clinical attachments and transportation to Petrograd would not have been cheap either.)

Following the Battle of Huj in November 1917, the WY presented the earl with a shell case. He had it exhibited in the *Advertiser*'s office. A small item appeared in 1919 in the *Advertiser* to the effect that the countess had sold some of her Essex estate for £97,017. She had no conception of money and foolishly believed that everybody was rich. She was seriously in debt in early 1914. As a former mistress of Edward VII when he was Prince of Wales, she unsuccessfully tried to get the Royal Family to help resolve her financial situation by selling the love letters she had received from Edward to them. When that failed, she was obliged to raise the money elsewhere.

Lord and Lady Brooke, Leopold Guy Francis Maynard Greville and Elfrida Marjorie Greville née Eden

Lord Brooke, son of the earl and countess and destined to become the 6th Earl of Warwick, was a professional soldier. During 1914–15 he was aide-de-camp for the British Expeditionary Force headquarters. By 1918 he had become a brigadier general of the 4th and 12th Canadian Infantry. After the war he left his wife and lived with his mistress in Mill Street. He died in 1928, believed to be from the delayed effects of neurasthenia.

Lady Brooke became involved in ambulance work and appealed for funds to provide a new ambulance train in France. The current one only had seven beds and the other wounded men had to lie wherever they could. She later became mayor of Warwick.

Henry Wheelwright and Agnes Marsh

Henry Wheelwright Marsh and his wife Agnes were wealthy American citizens. He was part of Marsh and McLennan Insurance Brokers and later their chairman. Aware of the earl's pecuniary problems, he and Agnes rented the castle for several months on an annual basis until 1926. Henry rented other properties in England when he was not back in America, where he was described as having 'very large business interests'. As the WY prepared to go to war, Mrs Marsh presented each man with a pair of gloves.

Henry returned to America in February 1915. It was fortunate that

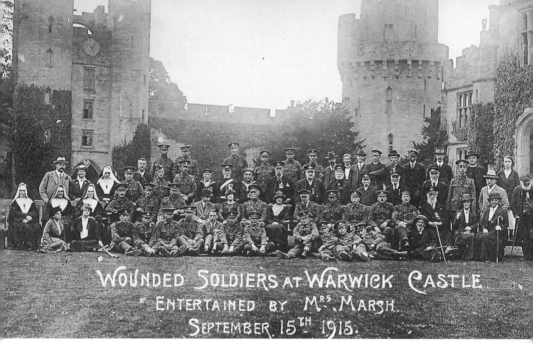

WOUNDED SOLDIERS AT WARWICK CASTLE
ENTERTAINED BY Mʳˢ. MARSH.
SEPTEMBER. 15ᵀᴴ 1915.

Mrs Marsh entertaining wounded men at Warwick Castle. (Author's collection)

he left when he did as he sailed on the *Lusitania* which was torpedoed in May of that year. During his absence, Agnes remained at the castle. A Harvard Medical Unit consisting of thirty-two doctors and seventy-five nurses visited her, when they were formally greeted by the mayor, sergeant-at-mace and the yeoman beadle. The latter two men were petty officers of WBC.

When she entertained a party of wounded soldiers from Coleshill, Agnes arranged transport for them. The wounded men were treated to dinner and tea plus entertainment. They entertained wounded troops from Birmingham and the WY in the castle during August 1917. A concert they arranged began in the county hall and finished at the castle for both the guests and the musicians, all of whom were blind. The event raised £51 14s for servicemen who had been blinded.

When American troops visited in 1918, they were well received by Warwickians, the mayor and Mrs Marsh. When the American Naval Secretary visited Warwick, he stayed at the castle. Following the Armistice, Henry arranged the return home for many American doctors and nurses still engaged in war duties.

Note:

Other buildings in Warwick used the name Castle because of the town's connection with the earls. W.J. Castleford became the new manager of the Castle Restaurant in Smith Street in early 1919. It would not be easy as the Ministry of Food was expected to continue operating until autumn of 1920. However, some relaxations were anticipated early in the year.

Castle Restaurant, Smith Street, Warwick. (Author's collection)

CHAPTER 16

Food Shortages

Importing food into Britain had never been a problem before because 'Britannia ruled the waves' but in 1914 that all changed as the war quickly developed. Throwing men onto the Continent and dealing with enemy surface shipping was one thing, but the German U-boats were something completely different. It took time for the government to realize the full impact of this new type of warfare.

Ultimately official rationing of food and other commodities was introduced, although a prior shortage of many items pre-empted this. Queues became an accepted way of life, although they were discouraged. Hoarding was also discouraged and later became illegal. People were exhorted to eat less and avoid wastage.

By 1916 the government was continually insisting on increased food production, but at the same time conscripting agricultural workers into the services. Less food being available meant a huge demand for it, leading to more money for retailers. Public information films concentrated on self-sufficiency. The Minister of Food Control, popularly known as the Food Controller (FC), took control of food supply and prices in June but many householders remained unconvinced that 'they had been adequately protected against unfair food prices'. As 1917 came to an end, war profiteers were warned that they faced imprisonment, not fines.

Food Production

Food production soon became a never-ending battle between the farmers and the government over prices and labour. The government demanded more food but continued to conscript its producers.

During the first week of the war in Warwick, the mayor insisted that there was ample food in the district and would be for some time to come. He condemned panic-buying but admitted that food would become more expensive. The mayor added a plea to 'the well-to-do to be generous to the not so well off. 'We must show that we are all united by the common ties of citizenship and brotherhood and resolved to make any sacrifice to defend the interests of our beloved country.'

Warnings followed about future shortages of agricultural labour. Many farmers were in the WY and already engaged in war duties, and their women were soon found running and working on the farms. The writing was on the wall and early in 1916 the government started recruiting 400,000 women specifically to work on the land.

Labour Shortages

Conscious of the labour shortage for the 1915 harvest, the government agreed that military help could be made available but only at the discretion of the local commanders. A Birkenhead schoolmaster advertised in Warwick that he was prepared to help with the harvest there. He did not want payment but expected his board and lodging to be free. The Eagle Engineering Company highlighted its equipment for haymaking.

Damage caused to farmland by military activities was inevitable, and farmers could make a claim against the War Office via the local military commander. The simpler claims would be dealt with first but applicants were warned that compensation 'was an act of grace' and not necessarily a right.

As the year ended, the Warwickshire War Agricultural Committee was started. Their initial function was to increase food production in the county and they needed to know the following:

a. What help was needed either in manpower or machines?
b. Which essential crop would be grown if such help was forthcoming?
c. Who would undertake to provide such help?

The Women's National Land Service Corps, usually called the Women's Land Army (WLA) started in March 1916, although farmers quickly objected to having women working on their farms. They

Wartime farming. (Public domain)

complained about not having enough labour, but then objected when help was offered.

However, Warwickshire was more realistic. The county had a big labour shortage and was unsympathetic towards such outdated chauvinistic attitudes. They were only too happy to accept all the help they could get. Only a week later, the first women began working on Warwickshire farms. Training was arranged in Warwick for those who would be employed locally. Warwickshire women were recommended to contact Miss Margesson of 12 Northgate Street, who was their local secretary. She arranged free training and provision of uniforms.

The RWR sent 225 soldiers back to England in June for work on the harvest. Farmer A.E. Bastock was not impressed by the replacement labour sent to him by the Warwick Labour Exchange. One of them was a tramp who 'did not agree with work' and the other was an epileptic. Mr Bastock had tried to keep his labourer on the farm and went to a tribunal in June where an exemption was issued but only until 1 August. Heavy rain also hampered the harvest.

Farmers warned that taking their workers could only lead to a decline in food yields. The government agreed and conscripting men employed in agriculture, dairy farming, market gardening and smallholdings was banned in October but not for long. The idea of using German PoWs was first suggested.

Early in January 1917 a meeting was held in Warwick to examine ways of increasing food production for the army. There were 1,800 Army Canteen Committees in the country responsible for the purchase of military food. The army promised to supply labour, usually in the form of PoWs. In spite of all these supply problems, the army had an insatiable appetite both for men and for food, yet made it clear that it would continue conscripting farm workers.

Before the month was out 50 per cent of all eligible farm workers were conscripted. Criticism soon followed. The government seemed unable to appreciate that fewer farm workers meant less food. A farmer with 400 acres had to manage with just 1 carter and 1 woman for 30 cattle, a team of horses and 300 sheep.

Field Marshal French entered the debate. He promised soldiers for help on the land during critical periods, provided that the farmers would speed up their work! However, he made no suggestions regarding how this could happen with the prevailing shortage of labour and machinery. According to the House of Commons, 'agriculture needs 200,000 more men just to maintain food production as in 1916.' Roman Catholics were permitted to carry out agricultural work on Sundays until the war ended.

As the food shortages began to be felt, WBC insisted that all available uncultivated land in the borough should be used for food production. Spring planting was behind because of the bad weather and a shortage of labour. In spite of imported food being seriously threatened by the U-boats, the government conscripted a further 30,000 men off the land, warning that more would follow. However, the release of soldiers to help with agricultural work had been so successful in Warwick that their return to active duty was delayed for a fortnight.

Warwick Castle Estate turned a field at Barford into allotments. It was believed that 60,000 acres in Warwickshire could be broken up for food production. In July sixteen new allotments became available and

WBC had two potato-sprayers for use within the borough. Potato production and protection figured in the public information films. West Gate Auctions sold excess vegetables etc. at their weekly Thursday sales, starting in August: 'Goods will reach good prices.'

A government instruction appeared in mid-September to collect horse chestnuts for production of acetone to be used in the manufacture of shells. This would replace starch that could be used for other purposes. Collectors received 7s 6d per cwt collected. However, more chestnuts were collected than could be transported and tons were left to rot. Warwickians collected 2 tons. Overall, the idea was not very successful.

Mr E.H. Webb, secretary of the Food Economy Committee at 11 Guy's Cliffe Terrace, had horses and tractors available for breaking up grass. As the year ended, the Food Production Department took over more than 20,000 badly-run farms all over Britain. Farmers had to obey orders for the breaking up of grassland. An agricultural depot opened near Warwick to help local farmers. It stored equipment and provided space for 300 horses, all of which were for hire.

Warwickshire farm workers were paid £1 10s per week which was fifty-four hours long from March to October and forty-eight hours in the winter. Overtime per day was set at 8¼d and 10d on Sundays. By March 1919 the fifty-four-hour week applied throughout the year. The Director General of Food Production resigned in protest. The National Farmers' Union found that the government's attitude to farming 'was parsimonious and niggardly and could only lead to less food, not more'. The current wage of £1 10s when compared with £2 in Scotland was not helpful either.

There was a big recruiting drive for the WLA that included a film at the Hippodrome and a rally in Birmingham. In April 1918 WBC made more land available for allotments, including 5 acres at the rear of All Saints School. The new allotment-holders demanded some form of security of tenure. In June a Warwick farmer was fined £20 plus £5 5s costs for failing to plough his land as instructed.

In a masterstroke of bad timing, the government conscripted a further 30,000 agricultural workers just before the harvest; they argued that the troops had to come from somewhere. Warwick farmers who employed disabled men under the age of 30 for less than £1 10s a week needed a permit from the Warwickshire District Wages Committee at

All Saints Church, Warwick. (Author's collection)

19 St Nicholas Church Street. It was proposed in August to make land available for discharged men. Common sense also seemed to have arrived when it was agreed not to call up any more 'key workers in agriculture'.

After the Armistice, applications for the release of serving soldiers for work on the land needed to be approved by the Board of Agriculture. Farmers who supplied their workers with milk and potatoes could only charge them the going rate and they could not charge more than 3s per week for renting a cottage. Early in 1919, the FC removed many restrictions on the distribution of cattle feed. Farm labourers now enjoyed a half-day holiday every week.

The Food Committee offered to supply horses and tractors to help with ploughing. With more men becoming available, 90 per cent of the soldiers still working the land were withdrawn. At the same time, the Warwickshire WLA was still in excess of 400 members strong and was described as being 'very active'.

Bread

By February 1915, the price of bread had risen from 7½d a loaf to 8d but it cost more in Germany. When November arrived, flour cost 1s a sack and loaves cost 9d. After the next price rise, the FC was heavily criticized because the flour was so adulterated that the price should have been dropped. Rolled oats for breakfast were suggested as an alternative by D. Massey, late Robinson & Sons, who sold them for 5½d per lb.

Conscious of the bread shortage, the government took over the large flour mills but complaints continued regarding the poor quality of bread. A Royal Proclamation requiring people to abstain from the unnecessary consumption of grain was read out in churches and chapels for four consecutive weeks. So many bakers were being conscripted in Warwick that the remaining bakers tried pooling their resources but the scheme did not work.

The FC promised to take action against anyone overcharging for bread and other items. He complained that too much bread was still being eaten but was quickly ridiculed: 'No one would have eaten an ounce of the present war bread beyond what was necessary.' It was that bad. Potato flour was suggested as an alternative.

In November, Herbert Tingey of 170 Emscote Road appeared in court again (his previous offence being in March concerning the sale of potatoes; see below). He was fined £2 for selling loaves that were less than twelve hours old.

It was felt in mid-1918 that supplies were safe until the harvest time. On the next anniversary of the war starting, bread production encountered another problem as conscription caused a serious shortage of bakers.

Butter, Cheese and Margarine

Pre-war butter cost 1s 1¾d per lb at Robinsons in Smith Street. Once the government realized that hostilities would not finish soon, they knew shortages of food and other commodities were inevitable. Part of their strategy was to bombard people with economic advice, such as using margarine instead of butter.

As 1917 ended, Town Clerk Mr H.C. Brown received new powers and quickly commandeered 10cwt of margarine from the Maypole Dairy in Smith Street and distributed it among the other shops in town.

However, the Maypole did not learn its lesson and in late January 1918 the town clerk seized a further 15cwt of margarine for redistribution. A queue had already formed when he arrived.

Cheese was still imported from America, Canada, Australia and New Zealand, and cost 1s 4d per lb. Farmers who sold their own butter did not need to be registered as long as they did not use retail premises. By February, a person's weekly ration was 4oz of butter OR margarine, and only registered customers could purchase from retail premises. Sugar and tea could be purchased elsewhere. Caterers were exempt. The end of the war led to an increase of 1oz per week but only for margarine.

Eggs

Pre-war Rhode Island Red eggs cost 2s 6d a dozen. The War Office appealed to the Warwick district in 1915 to provide 144 eggs per week for sick and wounded servicemen. The Wesleyan and other Sunday schools held egg collections that were donated to the local hospitals. A minimum of 500,000 eggs nationally were needed per week for wounded servicemen.

W.H. Webb advertised in 1916 that there was a fortune to be made from egg production, especially if you fed chickens on 'Karswood Poultry Spill containing ground insects which usually doubles egg output'.

Warwick Boy Scouts sent £10 12s 8d to London as their contribution to the National Egg Collection in late October. As the war ended, Westgate Girls' School donated £25 towards providing eggs for wounded soldiers. Eggs now cost 5¼d each.

Meat

The pre-war price of bacon was 9½d per lb at Robinsons. At their 1914 Christmas show, Margetts sold approximately 530 beasts. The Leamington, Warwick and District Master Butchers Association announced in May 1915 how they were 'reluctantly compelled to ADVANCE THE PRICE OF MEAT in all grades. And owing to a scarcity of labour, the PUBLIC are requested to place their orders a day in advance.'

WBC had problems with blocked sewers in June 1916, which had been caused by the disposal of animal entrails. Butchers were instructed to make other arrangements for disposal of unwanted animal pieces.

Warwickshire farmers protested in 1917 about the price of meat – £3 per cwt – which was fixed by the FC. In response he warned them not to be unreasonable by withholding their cattle requisitions.

By-law restrictions were relaxed regarding pigs to make more food available. All distributors of imported hams, bacon and lard must be registered by 14 December. The FC regulated how much meat would be sold before Christmas. All butchers threatened to close their shops after Christmas until concessions were agreed upon concerning the price of meat. The FC quickly met their demands.

Starting in January 1918, Warwick butchers shops were closed on Mondays, Tuesdays and Wednesdays. Wages were payable on Saturdays. Following protests by the Warwickshire Farmers' Union, the FC admitted that he had got the price of beef wrong.

By mid-March rationing cards were in the post and meat retailers had to register for all the types of meat they supplied, including game, cooked and tinned meats. In May, bacon and ham were only available from suppliers with whom the customer was registered. Men and women engaged in heavy manual work were entitled to supplementary rations but they had to apply for them in person.

The price of cattle was set at £3 15s per cwt and remained so until June 1919. Warwick allotment-holders now kept pigs on their land. By June, two food coupons were worth 1s 4d worth of meat. Smith Street butcher Frank Beech was fined £11 plus £5 6s costs for selling meat at a higher price than was permitted.

When the war ended, the meat trade was at the mercy of the Americans, who sent 'vile bacon at exorbitant prices'. The Ministry of Food agreed to make enquiries. The cost of all meat was later reduced by 2d per lb. Warwick butchers W. Hirons of Emscote Road and H. Stiles of Swan Street offered to buy porkers (young pigs) and cutting pigs (not yet castrated) at £1 8s per score (twenty).

Potatoes

The idea of growing vast quantities of potatoes arose in 1916. Seeing a commercial opportunity, the Eagle Engineering Company promoted its own goods and potatoes, referring to them as having 'great effectiveness against a disordered enemy'. WBC sold seed potatoes in 1917 to encourage residents to grow their own. Each customer was restricted to 5cwt. Farmers now complained that they were not being paid enough and they stopped growing potatoes. The government had to settle this dispute.

In March, Herbert Tingey of 170 Emscote Road sold 2lb of potatoes at 1¾d per lb when the correct price was 1½d. He was fined £1. Stocks were 'unusually low'. D. Massey promoted using rice instead of potatoes, available from him at 4d per lb. Potato disease was also a problem, so local authorities made sprayers available for smaller growers to borrow. The smaller sprayers were worn on the worker's back and operated by pumping a handle. Growers who hoped to make a profit were disappointed. Although permitted to charge up to £6 per ton, £3 or £4 a ton were more realistic prices.

The prime minister appealed for a further 1,000,000 acres of growing potatoes to be available during 1918. By April, Warwick bakers bought poor-quality potatoes to make bread. Even diseased potatoes could be made into flour once the affected parts had been removed.

Janet Talbot, a West Street grocer, was fined £5 for selling potatoes to a little girl if she also purchased a cabbage. Warwickian J.W. Bastock won £25 in the *Daily Mirror* potato-growing competition. He grew 509lb from 14lb of the Stirling Castle variety in his garden in Longbridge Road.

There was no let-up in restrictions in 1919. Only approved varieties of seed potatoes could be sold to or by authorized dealers.

Sugar

Pre-war Robinsons had sold granulated sugar for 1¼d per lb. The official price for sugar in 1915 was 4d per lb for granulated and 6d for cubes. Customers were encouraged to reports cases of overcharging. In February 1916, the Royal Commission on Sugar Supply promised to take drastic action against any grocer who refused to sell sugar 'unless tea or other specific articles are purchased at the same time'.

The FC recommended ¾lb of sugar per person per week in February 1917 but its supply was 'unsatisfactory'. It was expensive and poor people were unable to obtain any as shops tended to only sell it with other items, completely ignoring the FC's instructions.

Sugar-dealers had to register by 15 September. Sweetmeat dealers needed to be registered by the end of May 1918. In the weeks following the Armistice, holidaymakers were advised not to rely on purchasing sugar while they were away but to take their own. Restaurants were entitled to extra sugar.

Sugar: Bees
A.B. Wylie sold wooden and straw bee hives. By 1919 sugar was in short supply, although Warwick bee-keepers could obtain some from 12 Northgate Street.

Sugar: Jam
The government slowly realized that there was a vast amount of wild fruit available. When they did, children collected tons of blackberries for use in jam-making, the latter being always in demand from the army. By 1917 special bottles could be purchased for preserving fruit.

Serious concern arose in September 1916 because the lack of sugar meant that fruit was left to rot and jam manufacturers raised their prices. Jam-makers were advised to use benzoate as a substitute. This advice was quickly withdrawn as being 'not a good idea with serious results'. Benzoate was a food preservative that caused cancer and glucose was recommended instead. In June 1917 the Sugar Commission announced that it 'would try and make more sugar available for jam-makers'.

Wild fruit-pickers were paid 3d per lb in 1918. Among his numerous jobs, the town clerk dealt with applications for extra sugar other than for jam-making. An increase in the weekly sugar allowance came after the Armistice but it was too late for jam-making that year. Only after the peace treaty had been signed were jam-makers allowed to apply for extra sugar. Jam was still rationed in November 1919.

Pests
In mid-January 1916, twenty-two queen wasps were caught in the Castle gardens. The Warwickshire Hunt was criticized in April for not killing enough foxes. Organized pigeon shoots, aimed at reducing crop damage, started nationwide in 1917. If landowners and farmers declined, the Board of Agriculture and local authorities entered their land and destroyed the birds. Organized shoots held simultaneously across Warwickshire in 1919 proved more effective than individual ones.

Hunting. (Author's collection)

As most hunts had now ceased for the duration, foxes were shot to preserve livestock. Some of the troops, who had been released from fighting for ploughing duties, were now instructed to kill destructive game.

Rat and Sparrow Clubs were formed to combat the damage they caused. Young birds were shot in the nesting season. The Countess of Warwick disapproved of young children taking eggs from nests, in case they should fall. WBC offered a bounty of 2d per head for rats and 3d a dozen for sparrows' eggs. Rabbit damage was reported to 12 Northgate Street.

Rationing

It was soon realized that supplies of food and other commodities were not inexhaustible and people were warned to use less or face rationing. As 1916 progressed, fewer luxuries were imported as space on ships was needed for essentials. Stocks of tobacco were reported as being high.

With so many items being imported, the need for salvage became apparent. Girl Guides collected all forms of waste paper. Paper shortages meant that the *Advertiser* now printed smaller editions of the newspaper. In 1917 paper cost 4d per lb. In June the 'sale or return' system with papers and magazines was stopped. Newspapers remained small and expensive, and the *Advertiser* did not return to eight pages until 17 May 1919.

Already by January 1917 the compulsory rationing of food and other commodities was being considered. Critics warned that rationing had failed in Germany and would not succeed in Britain. In an attempt to delay/defer rationing, the FC recommended 4lb of bacon, 2½lb of bread and ¾lb of sugar per person per week. The Chamber publicly supported the FC in his endeavours to encourage voluntary rationing.

By April, food hoarding became illegal and so did selling food to hoarders. The police were empowered to examine business books and to raid private houses. On Empire Day in June, the government food proclamation order, as ordered by DORA, was read from the steps of the Court House.

Warwickians hoped that a voluntary scheme for rationing bread, cereals and flour would stop compulsory rationing being introduced. In some parts of the county, especially the rural areas, people were completely unaware of such a scheme. There were no plans as yet to compel shops to remove food from their window display and whitewash over the glass.

Another issue concerned children having enough food to eat and suggested introducing school meals for them. In another move to avoid compulsory rationing, the FC fixed prices. By October he demanded more economy or compulsory rationing would become necessary.

On New Year's Day 1918 the FC took control of supplies of oil, fat and potatoes. Compulsory rationing was inevitable. When it arrived in March, Warwick was already operating a local system along with Leamington, Stratford and Kenilworth. It was based on a similar scheme operating in Coventry. In Warwick a local food committee acted to prevent food queues. The FC wanted to stop what he described as the 'queue system'. He was told that there was no 'system' but when people heard of food deliveries they quickly descended on the premises and queues started to form. WBC wanted to minimize queues.

Food hoarders were an ongoing problem and they were duly prosecuted. An amnesty week encouraged hoarders to surrender their extra food without any fear of prosecution. It failed to reveal any hoards worth mentioning. However, there was no set definition of what was meant by 'hoarding'. Having more than one month's supply of home-

DEFENCE OF THE REALM.

MINISTRY OF FOOD.

BREACHES OF THE RATIONING ORDER

The undermentioned convictions have been recently obtained:—

Court	Date	Nature of Offence	Result
HENDON	29th Aug., 1918	Unlawfully obtaining and using ration books	3 Months' Imprisonment
WEST HAM	29th Aug., 1918	Being a retailer & failing to detach proper number of coupons	Fined £20
SMETHWICK	22nd July, 1918	Obtaining meat in excess quantities	Fined £50 & £5 5s. costs
OLD STREET	4th Sept., 1918	Being a retailer selling to unregistered customer	Fined £72 & £5 5s. costs
OLD STREET	4th Sept., 1918	Not detaching sufficient coupons for meat sold	Fined £25 & £2 2s. costs
CHESTER-LE-STREET	4th Sept., 1918	Being a retailer returning number of registered customers in excess of counterfoils deposited	Fined £50 & £3 3s. costs
HIGH WYCOMBE	7th Sept., 1918	Making false statement on application for and using Ration Books unlawfully	Fined £40 & £6 4s. costs

Enforcement Branch, Local Authorities Division,
MINISTRY OF FOOD.
September, 1918.

Breaches of ration orders. (Public domain)

produced items such as jam, eggs or vegetables was acceptable but purchasing a similar amount was not.

From mid-July 1918 a National Ration Book replaced meat and other ration cards. Application forms, which were completed as quickly as possible and returned to the local food office at 26 Jury Street, were being distributed. Grocers and other traders affected by rationing had a great deal of extra clerical work to do regarding food distribution. Unbelievably, some people applying for ration books failed to include their names and addresses.

The end of the war did not mean the end of rationing, which was expected to continue until at least June 1919. As if food and petrol rationing were not enough, hay was rationed in late August, with the army claiming priority. Following the Armistice, farmers faced continuing restrictions until February 1919 in being allowed to sell a maximum of 3 tons of straw to other farmers for thatching purposes. All straw usage had to be recorded.

National Kitchens and Communal Cooking

One of the ways of helping to ease the rationing problem coupled with reducing waste was the introduction of national or communal kitchens,

National Kitchens. (Public domain)

as promoted by the FC. However, the government went to great lengths to ensure that these kitchens were not the same as soup kitchens for the poor and needy. They were principally designed to reduce waste. In May 1917, the Tipperary Club gave food economy demonstrations. Cookery lessons were given at Westgate School.

December saw the beginnings of the first National Kitchen for Warwick planned for St Paul's old schoolroom in Theatre Street. By late January 1918, the kitchen had not yet opened because some of its equipment had not been delivered. Permission was needed from the Ministry of Munitions who were dragging their feet, despite the success of such kitchens elsewhere in the country. The necessary permits were given by the end of the month for four steam cookers that had yet to be manufactured! Examples of the food on offer were lentil soup at 1d, mutton pie at 3d, ginger pudding at 1d, beef croquettes at 2d, potatoes at 1d and rice pudding at 2d.

The kitchen was officially opened in late March by the Countess of Warwick and was very successful. At its peak it was described as being 'one of the best in the district'. By October, another kitchen was opened in Cherry Street. They both closed in early 1919.

CHAPTER 17

Drink

Non-alcoholic

In January 1914 RWR recruits visiting St Mary's were encouraged not to drink alcohol. By mid-1914 the British army was reputedly more sober than ever before. A licence was required for the pasteurising of milk. Alternatively it had to be boiled. One of the first hints of future restrictions came in November when the duty on tea was increased. The local branch of the Women's Total Abstinence Society took over the Theatre Street schoolroom in early 1915 for entertainment purposes.

Food and drink adulteration was a regular problem and not just a by-product of the war. Regular checks were carried out on milk-sellers as Stephen Green, dairyman of 21 Cherry Street, knew only too well when he was fined £2 2s plus 11s costs for selling adulterated milk again.

At its June meeting in 1916, WBC recorded that the average daily consumption and use of water in Warwick worked out at 20.15 gallons per person. Checking on milk samples could be a dangerous job. It cost WBC sanitary inspector S.T.W. White his life in June 1917 when he visited the cowsheds belonging to dairyman Eli Vernon, in the Banbury Road, to check for any adulteration. Vernon was an elderly man from Coventry Road who detested the inspector, having been prosecuted by him a few months previously for watering down his milk. When he saw White approaching, Vernon took his shotgun and killed him. Then he calmly reloaded his weapon and shot himself.

The price of milk rose from 1s 5d a gallon in October to 2s in November. The FC ordered the prices to be fixed and restricted deliveries when petrol rationing arrived. Deliveries changed in Warwick during mid-November when Bradbury & Romily of Cheshire took over supplying milk. They had fourteen depots and served 8,000 people. Local farmers refused to sell their milk for 6d when they could get 6½d in other areas. By the end of 1917, the maximum price of milk was 2s 4d a gallon.

After New Year's Day 1918, milk could only be sold in exact imperial measures. The quality of children's milk was reduced. Milk retailers had only a few days in which to register.

National consumption of tea was estimated to be in the region of 5,000,000lb per week. When a shortage of tea occurred, people believed 'it should never have happened'. Tea-drinkers needed to register with retailers before they could purchase their supplies.

Following the Armistice, the price of milk rose to 2s 8d a gallon. New restrictions in March 1919 banned serving milk in restaurants as a beverage. Ice cream could be sold as long as it did not contain milk cream. Tea-selling licences were no longer needed. Later that year, it was generally thought that women were better at milking than men.

Alcoholic

The war was a godsend for the Temperance Movement. Prime Minister David Lloyd George, himself a teetotaller, actively encouraged anti-drinking measures, sometimes backed by legislation. The duty on beer increased in November 1914.

Following what he described as 'a serious disturbance between the military and civilians' in mid-January 1915, the Warwickshire chief constable, backed by the military authorities, ordered all licensed premises including clubs to close at 10.00 pm. The report did not state where the disturbance happened.

By mid-October, King George V had declared himself to be teetotal for the duration of the war. Nevertheless, the Bishop of Oxford was disappointed that more people had not followed his example. The Countess of Warwick supported alcohol prohibition for women, but she had doubts about it also being applied to men.

June saw a rise in complaints from Red Cross hospitals in Warwickshire when convalescent soldiers were being bought drinks in local inns and were well intoxicated on their return to hospital. This practice was known as 'treating' and became a criminal offence. The chief constable threatened to bar patients from going out for a drink and the offending inns would be closed if the practice did not cease.

During the first week of 1916, beer and mineral water could not be supplied to billeted men. Bottled beers became more expensive. A few days later the Warwick licensing justices recorded a reduction in cases of drunkenness. At that time Warwick had 43 fully licensed premises, 8 beer houses, 3 grocers and 1 dealer who were licensed to sell alcohol in the town.

Harry Charles Smith, licensee of Ye Olde Three Tuns in Smith Street, was fined £50 plus £1 10s for two cases of 'treating'. The FC announced in 1917 that people must drink less wine, beer and spirits.

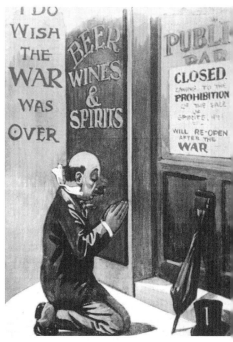

Praying for the war to end. (Author's colle...

In March, the Warwick Branch of the Women's Total Abstinence Union demanded total abstinence: 'The morality of the country would be purified if the facilities for drinking were removed.' This was quickly followed by a meeting at St Nicholas church hall where Mrs Creighton, a London widow, spoke on 'How to improve relations between men and war, blaming foolishness and giddy behaviour on Drink, Ignorance and want of recreational facilities.' Not to be outdone, in June the Reverend Wilson Stuart MA BSc lectured at the Northgate Wesleyan Church on 'Scientific and Political Revolution with respect to alcohol.'

Herbert William Gedge of the Plasterers Arms in Avon Street was fined £10 in November for selling beer at 6d pint when the correct price was 5d. He claimed he had not been told it was illegal.

In late January 1918, Lieutenants R. Corey Wright and Elliott of the RWR were cleared of being drunk in Middlesex. At the same time there was a growing demand for a national licensing scheme without local interpretations. An application was made in February for 18

Shakespeare Temperance Hotel, Warwick. (Author's collection)

Northgate Street to become a pub. The planners agreed, but only for the rear of the property as they thought a pub would be detrimental to the area. The Shakespeare Temperance Hotel, at the junction of 23 Market Place and 9 New Street, was for sale.

Publicans were warned in early March about not opening on time and discouraging off-licence sales. Days later it was announced that the 1918 beer was to be lighter and start at 4d a pint in bars.

George Bayley, another licensee of the Three Tuns in Smith Street, was fined £40 for selling diluted whisky 'at the excessive price of 6d' in early April 1919. Evidently the pub enjoyed something of a chequered career.

CHAPTER 18

Entertainment

Before the advent of television, people made their own entertainment, be it just for the immediate family or for larger audiences. With the arrival of wounded troops, there was a great need to help them pass the time while they recovered.

Numerous entertainments raised money for various causes while entertaining audiences. Many of the performers were amateurs, although military bands were sometimes involved. Critics complained about too much entertainment being provided for soldiers, but it helped to reduce mischief and drinking problems. Some entertainments were provided by soldiers themselves. Under what was known as the 'beauty sleep order', places of public entertainment closed at 10.30 pm.

The following are just some of the different forms of entertainment that took place during the war years and its immediate aftermath.

Balls

In January 1914 a Charity Ball held at the Shire Hall was attended by 400 people; tickets cost from 15s 6d. Later the Annual Children's Ball was held at the Court House, with participants wearing evening or fancy dress. Tickets cost from 3s.

Admittance to the Grand Victory Ball at Shire Hall on 10 January 1919 under the patronage of Sir Edward and Lady Nelson cost 12s 6d for double tickets and 7s for singles. Servicemen paid 5s. All the proceeds went to the Lance Corporal Vickers VC Testimonial Fund. People wore fancy dress or uniforms. It was the same order of dress for the Warwickshire Farmers' Ball held a few days later at the same venue. Tickets were more expensive, with doubles costing 17s 6d and singles 10s. Profits went to the Royal Agricultural Benevolent Institute and the Warneford Hospital.

Boating
From 1916, boating was permitted on the Avon on Sundays.

Boating at Warwick. (Author's collection)

County Hall, Warwick. (Author's collection)

Children's Parties
Shire Hall hosted a belated 1914 Christmas party for the children of local servicemen.

Cinderella Club
The club, part of a national organization founded in the nineteenth century to provide food and entertainment for poor children, met in November 1914 but the war meant no teas or entertainments for the children. Unfortunately the club was suspended until after the war.

Cinema
The Warwick Hippodrome opened in Edward Street soon after the war started. Their first film was *The Great European War*, with proceeds going to the Red Cross. It was followed by *The Adventures of Kathleen* which was serialized into thirteen parts and had cost £32,000 to make.

More war and patriotic public information films followed over the next few months, including some starring Charlie Chaplin. Some 230 wounded soldiers were entertained to a film show in January 1916. They were given pictures and cigarettes, and treated to a speech by the Earl of Warwick.

In common with cinemas all over the country, the official film about the Battle of the Somme was shown in September and was described as being 'the greatest moving picture in the world. It is impossible to think the world will ever forget this picture.' Families and friends saw some of what their loved ones were enduring. The showing was so successful that many people returned to see it again, which was hardly surprising as the RWR featured in it three times.

At about 10.25 pm on Wednesday, 1 November PC Turner discovered that the cinema was on fire. He raised the alarm and Fire Brigade Captain Richards with volunteers from the APC brought it under control by 2.00 am. Although arson was suspected, it could not be proved. Thanks to the fire brigade's quick response – they had been out on an air-raid alarm – the stage was not too badly damaged but other rooms were. Attempts to fight the fire were hampered because buckets of sand, supplied for such purposes, had been moved. John Henry Russell fell to his death here in February 1917 while carrying out post-fire repairs. The inquest verdict was 'accidental death'.

Children watched the film *The Warwick Pageant of 1906*, which had been directed by Louis Napoleon Parker. He was well-remembered in Warwick and elsewhere for his tireless work in aid of war charities.

During late November and December, the three films *War in the Air*, *War on the Sea* and *War on the Land* were shown. The last film of the year was *When Knights were Bold*. Most of it had been filmed at Warwick Castle, with some of the minor scenes taking place at Kenilworth.

The cinema was faced with possible liquidation in February 1918. Had the fire been arson? However, it survived, albeit under new management.

Louis Napoleon Parker (1906 Pageant director). (Author's collection)

Not a film show and definitely something that would not be tolerated today, the 'Budbrooke Darkies' held 'a Grand Nigger Minstrel Entertainment' that was followed by 'the screaming farce Black Justice.' All the proceeds were for PoWs.

In October the show [unclear if it was live or a film] was *The Better 'ole or the Romance of Old Bill* with Charles Rock playing the main role. 'Old Bill' was a fictitious cartoon character created by Captain Bruce Bairnsfather of the RWR, who appeared in the magazine called *Fragments from France*. The cartoons showed the life of soldiers in the trenches but with a comical/cynical appeal. Old Bill is best remembered for sheltering in a shell hole and saying to an approaching soldier: 'If you knows of a better 'ole go to it.' His cartoons were great morale-boosters.

Circus
Bronco Bill's Wild West Exhibition and Two-Ring Circus stood in the Hampton Road for two days in March 1914 and returned four years later.

Flower Shows
In spite of countless difficulties, flower shows continued, albeit with an emphasis on fruit and vegetables to encourage the home-growing of food.

Small circus at the Wheatsheaf Hotel, Warwick. (Author's collection)

Golf

A meeting in late November 1914 agreed that the Warwick Borough Golf Club should continue, although many of its members were serving in the war. Early in 1916 the Warwick Golf Clubhouse was commandeered by the military, although the links could still be used. It was wound up in October and a town club was formed in its place that needed £50 to £100 to take over the old facilities, with a further £50 per annum for club expenses.

An invitation was issued in 1917 seeking members. After 1 February a 10s joining fee was charged. Mr H. Smith-Turbeville became the first captain of the Warwick Golf Club, which soon became popular. Members of the APC who joined could pay quarterly.

In May 1919 a complaint was made, via the *Advertiser*, about the danger of golf balls hitting people walking nearby. This complaint was fiercely rejected by some golfers in an anonymous letter: 'Don't ask questions or you might get a tap on the head from this club. We West Street Boys want no gassing from anybody.'

Military Camps and Parades

These regular and popular events were well supported by Warwickians.

Music

In mid-1914, the 3/RWR camped on the race course where their band played publicly at 8.00 pm. Military bands became a great aid to recruitment, both into the RWR and the WY. Later, NCOs and men at Budbrooke Barracks were entertained by a band from the YMCA.

The scholars of the Brook Street Sunday School performed the operetta *Sunrise Land* in late April 1915. In early January 1916, Mr E. Roberts West gave the first of his organ recitals at St Nicholas church with Miss Marjorie Lees as his vocalist.

The WY gave a big military concert in January at Shire Hall that raised £18 for the Warneford Hospital. Unfortunately nobody had informed St Mary's Church, so their weekly bell-ringing practice coincided with the music. Churchwarden Mr J. Tibbits issued an apology and more concerts followed.

A choral event given by the APC Male Voice Choir at County Hall in May was a sell-out and raised £43 for the Warwick District Nursing Association. The APC gave several concerts during their stay in

Warwick racecourse. (Author's collection)

Warwick. Starting in 1917, the RWR Band played on Thursday evenings in the Market Place.

Soon after the Armistice, a concert was held at the Nelson Hall on behalf of the YMCA, under the auspices of the Coventry Co-op Education Committee and Warwickshire Advisory Committee. For undisclosed reasons the event was postponed for a week, possibly because of the Spanish flu.

Outings

In August 1916, the children from Castle Hill Sunday School were treated at the Asps by Mr Cockburn to tea, games and a cricket match. In the same week the choirboys from St Nicholas church were taken to Edgehill in a charabanc provided by the vicar. (The charabanc was an early motor coach version of earlier horse drawn transport using the same name.)

The 1917 annual outing for the Castle Hill Sunday School involved a picnic in the Hampton Road. The FC instructed them to bring their

Motor charabanc. (Author's collection)

own food which consisted of tea, two pieces of bread and butter, a bun and a cake but no sweets. It was described as 'being enough but not too much'. Parents also had to bring their own food.

Patriotic Entertainment
St Patrick's Night celebrations in 1917 were held in St Mary Immaculate Roman Catholic Church Hall and attended by numerous soldiers.

Sports
The APC annual sports day in August 1917 took place off the Hampton Road. Races included three-legged, egg-and-spoon, sack, old crocks and men over 40. Other events included a pillow-fight and 'tilting the bucket'. The latter was a burlesque of medieval jousting in which the steed was replaced with a wheelbarrow; if the 'jouster' failed to throw his pole through an overhead target, he and his barrow-pusher would most likely receive a drenching of water.

In the following month the Warwick and Leamington Garrison troops held their sports day, also off the Hampton Road. Their events included a baby show, decorated bicycle parade, military and ladies sports, and dancing in the evening.

Egg-and-spoon race. (Public domain)

Swimming

Special arrangements were made [not specified] in 1915 for the APC to use the baths in St Nicholas Meadow. Members of the WY used the baths during their recent training days in 1916. When the training finished, women used the baths between 6 am and 9 am on Mondays and Fridays.

WBC advertised in 1917 for a male attendant at the swimming baths in St Nicholas Meadow. The salary was £1 5s per week. In June the following year, a lady superintendent was needed to oversee the swimming baths for women for a few hours each week. The successful applicant had to be a good swimmer, able to instruct others and trained in life-saving. No salary details were shown.

In October WBC announced that the baths in St Nicholas Meadow and Priory Pools were closed [no other information known], possibly because of the Spanish flu.

Priory Pools, Warwick. (Author's collection)

Tipperary Club

In March 1917, the Tipperary Club collected blue and purple paper bags as used by grocers. These were in great demand for making splints for wounded servicemen. On Christmas Day 1918, ladies from the club delivered secret presents consisting of cakes, oranges, sweets and toys to 65 homes of war widows and 150 orphans. Unfortunately, two homes were inadvertently missed out but this was very quickly rectified.

CHAPTER 19

Financial

Warring countries continually need money, and plenty of it. With an ever-increasing demand for men, horses, motor vehicles, fuel, arms and ammunition, medicines, dressings etc., there was only one source from which money could be obtained: from the general public in the form of taxes, loans or generous donations. When taxes and expenses rose, so did prices and everybody was affected.

By mid-1915 the war was costing Britain £3,000,000 per day, while taxes raised only £750,000. By the end of 1916 the cost had escalated to £7,710,000 and six months later it was £8,000,000 per day, higher than had been forecast.

Only a few weeks after the outbreak of war, the size of banknotes was changed. Was this a move to prevent or foil a flood of enemy forgeries hitting the economy?

Banks
From 7 January 1915, banking hours remained the same except for Thursdays when they opened from 9.30 am. On Saturdays they closed at 4.00 pm. Closing time changed to 3.00 pm in 1917.

Big Gun Week
In 1918 WBC aimed to raise £60,000 from this fund-raising event involving a large artillery piece. It was scheduled for 11 to 16 November and £15,000 had already been pledged. Nelson Dale raised £10,000, provided the piece in question was an English gun and not German. The event was sponsored by Baker & Co. of Emscote, Lucas & Co. of Leamington and Warwick bookseller Henry Lacy. Every £5

collected paid for a 5in shell and every £1,250 paid for an 18in gun. Warwickians were encouraged to purchase savings certificates at the gun which would be located in the Square, with a prize draw at the end of the week. (This pre-arranged event then coincided with the Armistice. Reports were that it would still go ahead but further coverage ceased as the press obviously concentrated on the Armistice itself.)

Another money-raising scheme was to have tanks tour the country and collect money in the process. Warwick never had such a visit but in mid-February 1918 there was one at Coventry that had 130,000 visitors and raised £1,370,236. Undoubtedly Warwickians would have helped, had the tanks come their way.

Churches

Even the Church raised its taxes in 1917 when the most unpopular tithes went from £83 2s 6¾d a year to £92 1s ¼d. The tithes system was an unpopular tax levied by the Church for the benefit of the priest, who claimed one-tenth of all produced in the parish. Tithes were abolished in 1977.

The AGM of St Mary's Beauchamp Chapel Restoration Fund was held in July.

The shortage of coal in October 1918 meant that no more services would be held in any Church of England premises during the hours of darkness.

Clothing

The State took control of wool for the manufacture of uniforms in 1916 to stop inflated prices.

Coal

Charles Baker of Emscote Road sold coal from 18s 6d to £1 3s 6d per ton in early 1914. It rose by 1s in mid-December. More rises followed and local prices were regulated by WBC. As the war progressed, supplies became difficult to obtain.

A coal strike in Yorkshire was avoided when the miners' demands were met. Other strikes followed in different parts of the country. Yet the Warwickshire miners seemed to be less militant and in late April they received a substantial pay rise which they gratefully accepted.

Suggestions on how to reduce the use of coal included eating a cold meal at midday, using gas rings instead of fires and cutting down on waste generally. If the population only saved 1d a week per head, it would save £9,000,000 worth of coal.

By 1917 the attitude of many coal-miners in continually demanding more money angered the general populace. When a plan to recruit miners into the armed services failed, it was felt that they had a stranglehold on the country and the government was not prepared to upset them.

Coal deliveries were limited to 1 ton per household on each occasion. When rationing finally arrived in October, the allocation of coal was based on the number of rooms in the house. For example, properties of up to four rooms received 2cwt per week, while those of seven rooms received 1 ton per month.

Locally coal was in short supply and could only be collected at the Water Tower in Market Street on Mondays and Tuesdays; Baker's Wharf and Emscote Road on Wednesdays and Thursdays; and Priory Road Yard on Fridays and Saturdays. Coal cost 5d for 28lb, 10d for 56lb and 1s 8d for 1cwt. These arrangements were for ordinary people and not for dealers. WBC purchased a further 100 tons of coal to sell in small quantities during the winter.

In June 1918, while British soldiers were fighting fiercely at the front, 50,000 miners went on strike in South Wales. The general feeling in the country was that if they were not prepared to dig, then they should be made to fight. The colliers obtained another pay rise in July of 1s 6d per day or 9d if under 18 years of age.

More rationing of coal and coke followed but there would be extra available during the winter from the local fuel officer, Mr E. Melville Richards at 22 The Butts. He insisted the public must realize that there was a big shortage of coal. In May 1919 it was agreed to build a new power station by the canal bridge, where Tesco's now stands (in 2016), as being the only suitable place.

Collections and Flag Days

Street collections to help finance good causes started before, during and after the war, on a regular basis for local, national and allied causes. Flag days were instigated in 1914 by Agnes Morrison as a

*Charity pin.
(Author's
collection)*

way of raising funds for charitable causes by selling a small paper flag and pin for 1d. By 1919 the movement had raised £25,000,000.

Doctors
In 1915 doctors received 2s 6d for every military recruit they examined.

Donations
Within days of the start of the conflict, Mr Johannes Sauer, a refugee employed at the Eagle Works, was so grateful for having chosen Warwick as his home that he donated £10 for the poor.

Employment
Nelson Dale & Co. offered half-pay to all its married men who were on active service in 1914. War bonuses were given to some WBC workers in 1915. Married men earning £1 10s per week received a weekly increase of 2s and single men received an extra 1s.

WBC advertised in October 1916 for a beadle and town crier with a stipend of £1 1s per week. [When I took over that role in 1986, I was paid a weekly stipend of £1.25p (£1 5s), only slightly more seventy years later!]

The borough accountant was dismissed for fraud, although the money was repaid via a Fidelity Insurance policy. Later, William James Saville, then a private in the Army Service Corps, went to prison for six months for embezzling £10 11s 6d.

Just before Christmas, Warwick builders accepted a ½d an hour pay rise, although they had been offered 1d. Concern was expressed in 1917 regarding WCC bestowing benefits on members and employees. The WBC surveyor received a war bonus of 2s a week. In 1918 WBC needed a new borough accountant, overseer of the poor and poor rate collector, with a salary of £300 per annum with clerical assistance. The current holder of the post, Ernest D. Shepherd aged 37, had been conscripted and was only temporarily exempted until a replacement could be found for him.

Local farmers were encouraged to employ discharged officers for two years at £1 10s per week. In June, several workers at Nelson Dale went on strike for more wages and the recognition of the workers' union. However, not all workers supported the strike.

Gas
In the autumn of 1915, Warwick Gas Company raised its prices by 2d per cubic foot and warned of reduced supplies in the very near future.

Post Office
The ½d postage stamp was abolished in September 1915, making the minimum postage 1d. This move met with so much opposition that it was scrapped, but the cost of postal orders between 6d and 2s 6d rose by 1d.

Much concern was raised over the 'alarming rise' in the police postage account following the Military Service Bill in 1916. Later in the year Post Office Exchange Bonds were available for repayment in February 1920 at 6 per cent interest. They could be purchased for £5, £20 or £50.

The year 1918 was the busiest Christmas since 1914 and temporary postwomen were taken on locally to cope with the anticipated Christmas Day deliveries.

Victory Bonds
After the Armistice the mayor called upon Warwickians to purchase Victory Bonds.

Wages
In late January 1919 a serious complaint was made about two unnamed Warwick companies who had not paid the correct wages to munitions workers (no further details known).

War Bonds

These were another means of raising money and were reported as 'selling well' in October 1917. WBC invested £4,400 in the scheme but only a month later it was acknowledged that their sale was 'not as brisk as it could be, and Warwick needed to do better'. As 1918 dawned, Warwick lagged behind in expected War Bond purchases. The target was to raise £5,900 per week but in the previous fourteen days only £4,450 had been achieved. Leamington was also lagging behind. By late February, Warwick was raising £6,000 a week, or 10s a head.

War Bonds. (Public domain)

War Loans

In 1915, conscious of the ever-widening gap between the cost of the war and its funding, the mayor held a meeting in Leamington in support of the Great War Loan Movement.

War Savings Association

Warwick started its own local association in June 1916 as part of the National War Savings Campaign. It announced 'that everyone must save to help win the war'. The government offered small investments at high rates of interest. In the last quarter of the year, Warwick raised £893 1s 6d.

Warwickshire in Crisis Relief Fund
This fund was formed in late August 1914, with £5,500 being raised in the first hour. The fund aimed to help not just the families of servicemen but would include women. By the end of the month, £10,000 had been donated. There was little or no distress in Warwickshire at that time.

Widows' War Pensions
By November 1914 widows' pensions had risen: those with no children received 7s 6d; those with one child received 12s 6d; two children meant 15s; three children 17s 6d; and four children £1 0s 6d. A £5 gratuity plus a pension was paid to all widows whose husbands had been killed on active service since 1 July 1916.

Not a widow's pension but in a similar vein was that after the war, parents of fallen servicemen who were single could claim a pension if they were incapable of supporting themselves.

CHAPTER 20

Social

Life in Warwick continued with people living, dying and committing crime. New legislation brought an increased workload for the already overstretched authorities. When the police and other law enforcement bodies ceased to be exempt from conscription, fewer men had to do more work.

Crimes in General

It is impractical to try to list every crime, court appearance or other incident in this chapter. Neither is it possible to give any reliable statistics as their source cannot be guaranteed as accurate. For various reasons the final results were not always reported in the media. Supplies of paper were restricted, meaning that some items were omitted from the *Advertiser* and court proceedings could have been one of such economies. No doubt DORA also had an input into some reports.

The following figures are minimum numbers. Larceny, or theft as it is now called, accounted for 146 court cases; lights on vehicles came a close second with 134 cases; damage accounted for 92 cases; and drunkenness 81 cases. Other specific crimes will appear in their appropriate sections.

Accidents

In February 1914, Stephen Tibbits aged 8 was hit by a car at Eastgate when the motor scout who was responsible for traffic control was absent from his post, but fortunately Stephen survived. He came from a well-known Warwick family and went on to become a doctor and coroner in later life.

Eastgate with traffic scout. (Author's collection)

In January 1915, Percy Bosworth aged 7 of Cross Street fractured a shoulder after being knocked down in the Banbury Road by a cow. The danger of using candles was highlighted in April when Mrs Naylor of North Rock died after her bedclothes caught fire. Later the same month Miss Amy Elizabeth Gibbs aged 28 of West Street was gathering sticks and wildflowers when she was blown into the River Avon. Sadly she drowned as her astrakhan coat weighed 50 to 60lb when wet, making it too heavy for her to be able to climb out of the river.

The old did not always mix well with the new, as John Butler from Kenilworth discovered in November 1916. He was knocked unconscious with a gashed jaw after being thrown from his young horse when it reared at a passing tram.

Henry Bastock aged 66, a plasterer from Wharf Street, was killed in 1918 by a motor car in West Street. The car-driver, Mr J.H. Lambert from Leamington, was absolved of any blame. The deceased was deaf, drunk and had not looked before crossing the road.

Aliens (excluding Belgians)

In October 1914, aliens were instructed to keep the names they had at the outbreak of war and not to change them. Norman Edward Schwanke aged 16 was fined £5 in 1918 for incorrectly filling in his identity book. His father was a naturalized German.

The mayoress reported in September that her nephew Mr J.H. Lyon from Queensland was interned in Berlin as an alien. His wellbeing was monitored by the American Embassy.

Just before the first anniversary of the war in 1915, the Bishop of Worcester worried about German women marrying Englishmen in order to avoid being interned. He recommended that their banns should not be accepted in future without reference to the Registrar General.

In October, Charlotte Roberts of 5 Old Square was fined £10. She had failed to enter on 'a register to be kept for the purpose' the names and nationalities of all aliens over the age of 14 who were staying at her boarding house. The chief constable reported in January 1916 that there was a rise in the number of aliens registered in Warwickshire.

Assaults

In January 1919 Ernest Meredith, licensee of the Warwick Tavern in Crompton Street, was charged with threatening to kill his wife with a razor while he was drunk and fighting with their son. After three court appearances, he lost the licence which went to a Mr Antrobus.

Boots and Shoes

Starting on 7 June 1915, all Warwick boot-dealers closed their premises at 7 pm on Mondays, Tuesdays and Wednesdays. Early in 1916 the Territorial Force Association needed two working shoemakers to repair boots, which would be collected from the Corn Exchange. Six men were arrested in November and December for stealing army boots from there. Stealing military equipment or being in possession of it was a serious offence and they were each sent to prison for six months with hard labour.

Burglary

During a burglary in May 1915 at Warwick Railway Station, the safe was blown open and its contents stolen. Private William Fletcher of the RWR was charged with burgling The Vine public house in West Street the same month and stealing drinks and cigarettes valued at £2 5s 9d. He was acquitted at the Assizes.

Child Neglect

There was no shortage of offenders but this case in 1917 was the worst. Hilda Loot of 11 Coten End went to prison for four months, although she had denied neglecting her five children. When Dr Hubert Tibbits visited the house, he found insufficient utensils and bedding. The house was dirty, smelly, verminous and the children had been bitten. Three of the children were wearing dirty clothes. Hilda denied spending money with men, claiming that she always left enough for the children. She strongly denied taking men to bed with her. 'When have you seen me in bed with a soldier?' she demanded. 'Many a time,' replied her daughter Phyllis.

Civil Actions

In 1915 Ethel Annie Murdoch, a domestic servant, successfully sued Thomas A. Bayliss from St Johns for £1 18s 4d owed to her for wrongful dismissal. Suffering from an injured back, she had refused to carry her master upstairs and was dismissed. He died later in the year and left an estate worth £42,528 19s 5d.

St John's House, Warwick. (Author's collection)

Later that year, Austin Edwards was unsuccessfully sued for libel by the Hepworth Manufacturing Company. Austin Edwards had written saying they would not do any more business unless the agent was paid a commission.

Death on the Home Front

Joy Loveridge committed suicide in October 1915 after having an affair with a married soldier. The coroner stressed that the inquest 'was not a court of morals'.

In February 1916 an inquest held on Frederick Turner, a labourer at Nelson Dale & Co., found that he had died from anthrax. The jury decided that no one was to blame for his death. It was agreed the same month that the grave of Warwick hero Sergeant Richard Perry in St Mary's churchyard should have a proper headstone. He had died in 1855.

During March, William Worsley was found dead in his allotment shed in Charles Street where he had led a 'Robinson Crusoe-like existence for the past two years'. The coroner was concerned that he had not come to the notice of the authorities.

April saw the inquest held on William Chaplin aged 51 of Knowle Villa, 81 Coten End. He had died from gas poisoning in his bedroom with the gaps around the windows and doors covered. William was a lifelong invalid who suffered from depression. Clearly it was suicide, tempered with the rider of 'temporary insanity'. Margetts handled the auction sale of the house effects on 16 November following the death of Mrs Chaplin. (I lived at this address for a number of years but had no knowledge of this sad event.)

The estate of the late Bertha Aletha Hill, granddaughter of the late Robert Southey, included four Gainsborough paintings that were sold for 3,250 guineas (£3,412 10s). Her grandfather had been one of the Lake Poets and Poet Laureate for thirty years. She had been one of Warwick's oldest residents, living in Church Street, who died in February 1917 after falling onto the fire while she was dozing.

A sad inquest in late September 1918 involved Dorothy Mabel aged 14, the daughter of Councillor and Mrs Kendall of Northgate Street, who died after drinking nitric acid. She enjoyed a friendship with Annie Cracknell, which her parents had forbidden. It is unclear what happened except that Dorothy had found some nitric acid in her father's yard. The jury returned a verdict of 'Death by Misadventure'.

Mrs Emily Maiden aged 59 was found dead of pleurisy, hypothermia and starvation in her verminous home, 56 Pickard Street, in November. She was nearly blind, had practically no bedding and dressed in some old clothes and a few sacks. Being a proud woman, she refused to accept any charity but survived on her pension and the earnings of her 16-year-old child. Mr John Tibbits ensured that the health authorities were informed.

The death was announced in November of George Cattell Greenway at Ashorne Hill. The *Advertiser* described him as 'a man of great charm', omitting to mention how he had gone to prison for five years for fraud while he was Warwick's town clerk in 1888.

George Greenway (left) on trial. (Author's collection)

In February 1919, Private John Henry Garrett died in Wharf Street from disease he had contracted while on military service. He was given a full military funeral at Warwick Cemetery. A few weeks later, former Quartermaster Sergeant Samuel Brison aged 81 died. He had lived in Warwick for a few months, having served during the Crimean War and the Indian Mutiny.

Disaffection

In late December 1916, conscientious objector Joseph William Illingworth went to prison for two months with hard labour. He had made verbal statements prejudicial to recruitment and other comments likely to cause disaffection among troops. When questioned by plainclothes police, he replied: 'I don't work and the government can't make me.' That attitude would not have been tolerated in prison.

Fire Brigade

Members of the brigade participated in parades, etc. They were based in The Butts and in January 1914 advised their scale of charges for attending at fires outside the town: engine appliance 6s 6d; captain/lieutenant 5s or 2s 6d; and 3s for the crew.

Fire brigade. (Author's collection)

Their attendance at a farm fire in Wasperton was hindered because one of their horses had been taken by the army, and aggravated while another one was brought from the Warwick Arms. Then extra horses were needed because of the distance. The fire caused £1,000 of damage to a farm that was owned by St John's College, Oxford. WBC purchased another horse for the fire engine.

Due to worries about causing any possible alarm regarding air-raids, it was agreed in 1918 to summon the brigade by maroons in the daytime. A conference of Midland Fire Brigades agreed to mutually support each other if necessary.

Fraud

Criminals were quick to take advantage of the immediate rush of patriotic enthusiasm. People were warned only to give money to bona fide National Relief Fund collectors as fraudsters were already making money in this way.

Housing

The provision of sufficient housing is no new problem. Poor living conditions always constituted a health problem for WBC, who made regular health visits to the poorer parts of the town. When appropriate, they issued closure orders on some properties as being unfit for habitation. In 1914, WBC agreed to close houses in Friars Court, Monk Street and Chapel Street unless they were made more habitable.

WBC reported in June 1915 that more old houses had been cleared since 1911 than new ones built. They had inspected 173 houses, of which 146 needed immediate repair and 10 were condemned because no attempts had been made to repair them. A Warwick man serving in India during 1918 wrote to the *Advertiser*: 'I see that after the war they intend to build a lot more homes in Warwick. I am glad that Warwick is beginning to wake up.' Within days of the Armistice, three sites were being examined with a view to building 4,150 houses on them. By early January the plans took shape, with twelve houses planned to the acre. Sites were identified on the Hampton Road; the Deer Shed (off Cape Road opposite the Pigwells); and Emscote Road at the rear of Humphris Street, Bridge Street and All Saints Road.

Indecent Assault

In 1917 Private Ernest Clarence Hayes, APC, was sentenced to six months' imprisonment on each charge of assaulting two boys, the sentences to run consecutively.

Lighting Offences

With so many extra troops in the area, there was an increase in bicycles being used, often at night and without displaying any obligatory lights. It was a similar situation with motor vehicles. Not blacking out buildings at night was a new offence. Some people treated these regulations with contempt because Warwick was not a high-risk area for air-raids. However, their views did not prevent them being prosecuted. Offenders came from all walks of life.

A meeting of WBC in January 1916 stressed the need for all council-owned property to comply with the lighting regulations. A committee liaised with the police on which lights could be left on. Grocery shops closed earlier so as not to run the risk of lights being seen. As the year ended, white bands were painted around lamp-posts to make them more visible in the dark.

On 21 May 1916 Daylight Saving arrived and it never went away. While WBC agreed to abide by it, there was much opposition nationwide. One critic wrote 'it could only come from a cranky and fermented brain of a candidate from a lunatic asylum... Why not get up an hour earlier?' Farmers in neighbouring Northamptonshire agreed 'to ignore this sham time and go by the sun'.

Police

At the January 1914 meeting of the SJC, which oversaw the police, Chief Constable Captain John Brinkley asked to increase his establishment by 1 extra inspector, 2 sergeants and 23 constables. He actually needed forty men to cover the deficiencies caused by the new rest-day rotas. Little did he know then that during the course of the next few years, he would have fewer staff to carry out more duties. By June, police recruits needed to be a minimum of 5ft 9in tall and were paid between £1 7s and £1 15s per week.

The constabulary donated £50 to the County War Fund in November. Female police constables were appointed at Southampton in 1915 but Warwickshire did not follow suit until 1941. In May

Old Warwickshire Constabulary Headquarters. (Author's collection)

married men received an extra 2s per week and single men an extra 1s. Provision was made for officers who had lost leave days when the war started to be recompensed by an extra four days during this year, but 'only at the discretion of the chief constable'. During the same month, seventeen Germans who lived in Warwick were arrested and interned.

The chief constable reported to the SJC in January 1916 that the constabulary was now seventy-eight men below its authorized establishment. In July the SJC stated that 'we do not consider the present abnormal times appropriate for readjusting salaries or allowances.' Nevertheless, they increased the superintendents' horse allowance from £60 to £75 per annum and ensured that they would now receive the same bonuses enjoyed by the other ranks.

At the January 1917 meeting of the SJC, one councillor thought that more police should be called up. He was advised that the force was already ninety men under establishment. The April meeting agreed to increase bonuses by 4s a week for inspectors and 3s for sergeants and constables. In October Superintendent Ravenhall became the new deputy chief constable and there was a further increase in bonuses.

Police Superintendent James Ravenhall. (Author's collection)

The Warwickshire Constabulary acknowledged that they had a duty to assist enforcement of the food orders made in 1918 but declined to do so. The task was far too big for their limited resources. Communities had to fund their own enforcement officers.

Early in January 1919, PC Turner was demobbed and returned to duty at Warwick. The SJC agreed that police officers who had been discharged from the Colours on medical grounds and who were below the normal standard for police recruits should be retained on light duties. The SJC became involved in the house-building plans at its April meeting by stating that more police houses were needed in Warwick.

Pornography
Ben Shaw of the RWR was sentenced in 1916 to one month in prison for sending an indecent print through the post to Miss Isabella Kirk.

Post Office
WBC disapproved of the Post Office linking Warwick and Leamington together in 1919. They felt it 'not very dignified' for a county town and a military centre.

Prison
On 1 June 1916, the gaol closed for the duration of the war and the

*Warwick prison main
entrance. (Author's collection)*

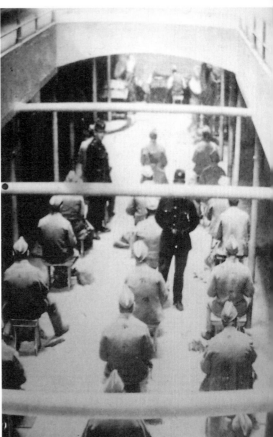

*Inside Warwick prison.
(Author's collection)*

prisoners moved elsewhere. It was returned to being a prison after the war.

In October the gaol, soon to be known as 'the Settlement', housed conscientious objectors, who worked on the premises making boots, tailoring, growing vegetables, etc. If they absconded, they could be sent to prison, be returned to their original prisons or sent to the army. Complaints were received in 1917 about lights being seen in the night, contrary to blackout regulations.

Risk of Burning
In January 1914, a Warwickian was fined £10 for leaving a child under 7 years of age in a room with an unguarded fire.

Theft
Site foreman George Skeet and haulier Edwin Ludlow from Stand Street were each fined £10 in August 1915. They had stolen 164lb of copper wire valued at £7 7s that linked the pumping station to the Warwick Arms. Private William Yardley was sent to prison for three years with hard labour for stealing property from dead soldiers in 1918. However, his sentence was halved on appeal.

Warwick Borough Council Miscellaneous
In May 1915, WBC stated that it would give preference to applicants seeking employment after the war who had served their country either in the military or in engineering. The town clerk, Mr Brabazon Campbell, resigned in 1917 for a younger man who would be better able to cope with extra duties.

On the third anniversary of the outbreak of war in 1917, WBC resolutely supported Britain's determination to continue the war 'to a victorious end'. After the meeting, members went to a service at St Mary's. In mid-June 1918, the town clerk appeared in public for the first time wearing a wig and gown, and town clerks still do so today.

Workhouse
Before the war started, the mortuary was criticized as being in a poor state and needing attention. Children were kept out of the workhouse by placing them with foster parents. A labour mistress was wanted in May 1915 for a salary of £20 per annum plus accommodation, rations

and washing. Christmas dinner that year was roast beef, roast potatoes and parsnips followed by plum pudding and custard sauce. Oranges, apples, tobacco, tea and beer were also available.

During 1916, the BoG protested about the growing numbers of lunatic soldiers being admitted and blamed government policy. The 1916 Christmas lunch was similar to 1915, but the men were restricted to 6oz of beef plus vegetables and 6oz of plum pudding accompanied by one apple and one orange. Women had a pint of coffee or cocoa and only 5oz of beef; otherwise the menu was the same.

During 1918 the government proposed to abolish the BoGs. Sunday meat was now reduced to 2oz with 4oz of vegetables per resident and no bread. More vegetable pies were provided, with pickled herrings on Friday. The master was instructed to reduce food consumption, either voluntarily or compulsorily.

CHAPTER 21

Peace at Last

Although the Armistice began on 11 November 1918, the war did not officially end until 28 June 1919 with the signing of the Treaty of Versailles. With certain exceptions, such as agricultural workers, the country remained on a war footing with many men still abroad, albeit in less danger. This delay was caused by the Germans refusing to accept that they had lost the war.

Nevertheless, for most people back home the war had ended in 1918 and they started to rebuild their lives. It was a time for rejoicing and remembering. With more than 200 Warwick men having lost their lives in the conflict, many families struggled to cope in the aftermath.

Obverse Victory Medal. (Author's collection)

Reverse Victory Medal. (Author's collection)

Armistice

Even before Monday, 11 November 1918 arrived, people knew that the end of the war was imminent. Germany's allies had been defeated and American troops flooded into France. Crowds had already gathered in Warwick; not just for the news, but also for the arrival of the big gun for fund-raising. When it arrived, the prime minister's telegram was posted up in the *Advertiser* office window in the High Street: 'You are entitled to rejoice. The people of this Empire with their Allies have won a great victory. It is the sons and daughters of the people who have done it. It is a victory greater than has ever been known in history.'

The town erupted with church bells ringing and flags being waved by children everywhere. I remember how I waved my flag when Germany surrendered in 1945, although I was living in Leamington at the time. No great celebrations were planned as this was only the Armistice, although a straw effigy of the Kaiser was hung from the tram wires in the High Street. A large crowd joined the mayor and councillors in the Square with the big gun. Large congregations filled the churches and celebrations continued into the night and well into the next day. Chinese lanterns were lit all over Warwick.

On Thursday evening, the mayor and civic leaders attended a special thanksgiving service in St Mary's, which was decorated with flags and flowers. The hymns included *Praise, My Soul, the King of*

St Mary's Church, Warwick. (Author's collection)

Heaven and *O God, Our Help in Ages Past.* The organist played the *Hallelujah Chorus.*

The mayor later received a captured German gun from the RWR, which was put in the Square. Complaints were soon received about children playing on it. An attempt to move it into the Pageant Gardens failed because it was too wide to pass through the gate.

Peace in 1919

The Germans continued to prevaricate and cause delay. Nevertheless, towns and cities prepared to celebrate the peace. No plans were made in Warwick until the town clerk informed WBC in May that if they 'did not have any peace celebrations, it would the only town not to'. When the news of the final peace was received on the Saturday, church bells were rung, flags were flown and a bonfire lit in Friars Street. However, there was no great excitement in the town.

On the following night some drunken soldiers dragged the captured gun to St Nicholas Meadow and pushed it into the Avon while a large crowd cheered and encouraged them. The mayor was given another gun which he hoped would not suffer the same fate. This gun had come from Gaza. Eighty years after the Battle of Huj, one of the captured guns was presented to the WY museum.

River Avon, Warwick, where the captured German gun sank. (Author's collection)

Saturday, 19 July marked the official peace celebrations throughout the country, although there had been a children's tea party and entertainment in the Castle Park on the previous day. The actual day started fine but ended wet. At noon, dinners were held for returned soldiers and sailors at the Corn Exchange, County Hall and Portobello Inn. These were followed by sports, dancing and a firework display. Cherry Street held its own celebrations in the youth club which included a jazz band. Brook Street hosted a tea and dance. A tea was provided at Budbrooke Barracks for 400 warrant officers, NCOs, men and their families. Yet there was a marked lack of enthusiasm everywhere with no spectacular displays. The weather did not help and there were many bereaved families in Warwick.

Post-war Employment

In June 1918, a Warwick Disabled Sub-Committee was set up to help servicemen needing treatment, training and advice. Later it included discharged and demobilized troops. It was operated from 13 Old Square (home of the Tipperary Club) by Lieutenant Colonel R.E. Negus.

Within hours of the Armistice the committee realized that there would be conflict between demobilization and industrial reconstruction. The situation was not helped by various changes to the demobilization plans. As anticipated, conflicts soon arose between men expecting to get their old jobs back but found that they were being done by women, who had then tasted independence and had no intention of returning to domestic service. Disabled men wanted to preserve their dignity but were obviously restricted in what work they could undertake. The women made the valid claim that they too had families to feed. The APC in Warwick was one example.

Field Marshal Douglas Haig highlighted the shoddy way in which returning servicemen were being treated regarding their pensions and gratuities. Officialdom was callously indifferent and medical boards considered many claimants to be malingerers. The situation was aggravated by the final signing of the Treaty of Versailles and the speeding up of demobilization.

Disabled servicemen who wished to have further instruction in the use of their artificial limbs were advised to contact the local pensions office nearest to where they lived.

War Memorial
In December 1916, although the end of the war was nowhere in sight, it was proposed to erect a shrine in some prominent place to honour the Warwickians who had lost their lives in the conflict. The original memorial plaques were made of wood. People who wanted their loved ones to be remembered had to inform the mayor via the *Advertiser*.

Royal Warwickshire Regiment memorial in St Mary's Church, Warwick. (Author's collection)

Warwick war memorial in Church Street. (Author's collection)

When the memorial plaque was unveiled in Church Street in March 1917 by Lady Nelson, there were over 100 names on it. The event was witnessed by a great crowd and was a very moving event: 'One poor woman, the tears streaming down her face, came to offer her bunch of snowdrops in the memory of some brave boy whom she had lost.' The original plaques were attached to the iron railings around the Church Street side of the churchyard. By April 1919 there were more than 200 names on it. At that time, no firm plans regarding the site and style of the town's memorial had been made. William Bull was fined £1 for stealing flowers from the shrine.

A committee, appointed in May 1919, quickly reported that they 'could not afford anything very magnificent' but thought 'they can get something that will endure'. Suggestions included a river walk, memorial to include a gun, an Old Comrades' Club, public baths, and turning the Pageant House into a dancing salon. The Bishop of Coventry recommended that the memorial should be a perpetual memory to the fallen rather than to serve some local need, and preferably with some sort of religious connection such as a cross. He also reminded people that nobody had the right to a wall space in church for a memorial tablet.

The war memorial was finally sited in Church Street where it still stands today. Only a few years ago, more names were added to it. A memorial to the RWR is in St Mary's Church.

Conclusion

In spite of everybody supposedly pulling together, this was not always the case. Clearly the military ruled the government with their insatiable demands for more men. The government did as it was told where the military were concerned. A similar situation involved many miners and railway workers who always appeared to get what they demanded. It caused a great deal of ill-feeling in the rest of the country. Possibly the government had no alternative as coal was needed for all manner of purposes including running trains.

How could the government reconcile its conscription of essential men, such as farm workers and shipbuilders, yet still demand more food? Who was going to provide it? How many members of the government knew what farming was all about? Then the farmers did not really help themselves by demanding more help but refusing to use women and PoWs. Such actions did nothing to further their cause in trying to keep workers from being conscripted. The farmers were born in Victorian times and still lived in that era where women had no independence and supposedly no thoughts of their own. Perhaps they had a bit more of an argument when it came to using German PoWs and consequent fears of being murdered. I have to stress that Warwickshire farmers were more far-sighted and were only too grateful for assistance, regardless of its origins.

Then there was the attitude of the Education Committee who resented and opposed children working on farms. No doubt its members were more than happy to eat the food, as long as their private empires were not affected. Expressing concern about the loss of education was their way of protesting.

The medical fraternity objected to Red Cross volunteers helping in the hospitals but who else could tend the wounded? Other people objected to the blackout regulations and flouted them because it did not suit them to comply.

How could a French polisher and Lord Willoughby de Broke's secretary be exempted from military service when other more deserving individuals were conscripted? I suspect it all came down to who you knew.

Theoretically, Britain's population might all have been in the war but their contributions varied tremendously. There was no shortage of critics whose private little empires were disrupted by the war's demands, yet none of them came up with any suitable alternatives. For many of them it was a case of it not being their job. It all tends to emphasize how various groups were only interested in their own needs.

What happened in Warwick tended to mirror the rest of the country. Warwickians played their part in this war both at home and abroad. Many of them had their lives changed for ever, all because of the Kaiser's ambitions.

The 'war to end all wars' ended on 28 June 1919 with the signing of the Treaty of Versailles which imposed harsh terms on the Germans. Just over twenty years later, hostilities with Nazi Germany began (the Nazi Party having been founded in 1920), all because of Hitler's ambitions which had not been deterred by the previous conflict. It proved the truth in the old saying that the only lesson of history is that nobody ever learns the lessons of history. More names would be added to the war memorial.

Bibliography
and Sources

Publications

Black's Medical Dictionary

'The Eventful 20th Century: The War to End Wars 1914–1918', *Reader's Digest*

The Warwickshire Yeomanry (Warwickshire Yeomanry Museum)

Warwick Town Council Minutes

Anand, Sushila, *Daisy: Life and Loves of the Countess of Warwick*

Beckett, Ian, *Home Front 1914–1918: How Britain Survived the Great War*

Bristow, Joy, *The Local Historian's Glossary of Words and Terms*

Doyle, Peter and Walker, Julian, *Trench Talk: Words of the First World War*

Ellis, John, *Eye-Deep in Hell: Life in the Trenches 1914–1918*

Hamilton, Andrew and Reed, Alan, *Meet at Dawn Unarmed*

Hamilton, Robert, *The Great War: Unseen Archives*

Hayward, James, *Myths & Legends of the First World War*

Higginbotham, Peter, *Workhouses of the Midlands*

Holland, Chris, *Before Gallipoli*

Howe, David, *Willingly to School*

Lang, Theo, *Darling Daisy*

Longmate, Norman, *The Workhouse*

Moore, Peter, *Damn His Blood*

Rankin, Nicholas, *Churchill's Wizards*

Reilly, John, *Policing Birmingham*

Richardson, E., *History of Budbrooke from 1122–1968*

Smith, Mark, *The History of the Royal Warwickshire Regiment*

Stevens, Philip, *The Great War Explained*
Sutherland, Graham, *Bloody British History ... Warwick*
— *Dastardly Deeds in Victorian Warwickshire*
— *The Warwick Chronicles 1813–1820*
— *The Warwickshire Beat 1877–1912*
Swingle, S.L. and Turner, K., *The Leamington & Warwick Tramways*
Waters, Colin, *A Dictionary of Old Trades, Titles & Occupations*
Wilmott, H.P., *First World War*

DVDs
Public Information Films of the British Home Front
The Battle of the Somme

Organizations
Leamington Library
Royal Warwickshire Regimental Museum
The Cardall Collection at Southam
Warwick Advertiser and *Warwickshire Advertiser*
Warwick Visitor Information Centre
Warwickshire County Museum Service
Warwickshire County Records Office
Warwickshire Yeomanry Museum

Other Sources
John Ashbourne
Graham Doughty
Alan Reed
Alan Sturley
François Wicart

In particular I would like to thank Phillip Wilson for all the help he gave me concerning the role of the Warwickshire Yeomanry during this conflict.

Index